# SINGING

# Da Capo Press Music Reprint Series

MUSIC EDITOR
## BEA FRIEDLAND
*Ph.D., City University of New York*

# SINGING

*A Treatise*
*For Teachers and Students*

By

HERBERT WITHERSPOON

DA CAPO PRESS · NEW YORK · 1980

Library of Congress Cataloging in Publication Data

Witherspoon, Herbert, 1873-1935.
  Singing.

  (Da Capo Press music reprint series)
  Reprint of the ed. published by G. Schirmer, New
York.
  Includes index.
  1. Singing. I. Title.
MT820.W48  1980  784.9'3            80-12944
ISBN 0-306-76001-0

Published by Da Capo Press, Inc.
A Subsidiary of Plenum Publishing Corporation
227 West 17th Street, New York, N.Y. 10011

# SINGING

## *A Treatise*
## *For Teachers and Students*

By

# HERBERT WITHERSPOON 1873–1935

✣

Price, $3.00

X 157

## G. SCHIRMER, INC.
### New York

To
*My Mother*

Whose self-sacrifice, ambition and perseverance
helped make my education possible,

*And to*

*My dear Wife, Florence Hinkle*

Who by her own singing has proved many of the
principles contained in this little volume,
I dedicate this book.

# CONTENTS

## PART I

The object of art is expression.
The essence of expression is imagination.
The control of imagination is form.
The "medium" for all three is technique.

# SINGING

## PART I

### CHAPTER I

**The Purpose of this Book—Dangers of Specializing—Technique and Expression are Inseparable**

THE human voice has been a subject of investigation for many years. This investigation has become more and more specialized as the years have gone by. A great danger in this investigation has been the centering of attention upon certain parts or "locals," with a corresponding loss of attention to general and sympathetic coördination. This is true of the specialized study of anything pertaining to the human body.

The history of past and even ancient investigation of the human voice shows the same tendency, and is a matter for encouragement in this respect, because we find this specializing in evidence from the very beginning of singing. In the time of the ancient Greek orators and actors several "fads and fancies" originated, some of which are curiously ingenious, some even alarming in their practice.

We all know the story of Demosthenes and his "mouthful of pebbles" and we may be amused thereby; but we may be a little alarmed when we read that actors of Greek tragedy slashed the back of the throat, the pharynx wall, with sharp instruments, in order to cause an irritation and ensuing "granulation" of the membrane, in the belief that this condition of sore throat increased the carrying power of the voice.

So we find even in the beginning of the art of singing, for the Greek actor was at least half a singer, the inclination toward queer tricks as imaginary "local" aids to the production of voice.

Perhaps because the singer is dealing with the half-seen, because his instrument is part of his own body and self, this search after special action has gone on and on through century after century, each "cog of the wheel" being examined and specialized upon, until natural law of coördinate physical action has become largely lost in a maze of detail leading only to confusion.

1

The subject in hand is a difficult one, but in my opinion it has been made more difficult than is necessary, because it has been surrounded by all kinds of mystery and over-analysis which have not led to reconstruction of ideas into definite form and laws. There would seem, therefore, to be a need of a book, somewhat in the nature of a text-book, useful alike to teacher and pupil, which will show the natural laws governing the voice organs, the established and accepted facts upon which these laws depend, the best means of insuring obedience to these laws, and the faulty results due to disobedience. I have been a close student of the existing literature on the human voice, but I know of no such book.

I would divide the existing books treating of the singing voice into three classes:

(1)  Those which are or attempt to be purely scientific.
(2)  Those which are frankly empirical.
(3)  Those which engage both attitudes of approach.

The first class has given us to a large extent the "local effort" school; the school which teaches to stress certain acts with definitely separated organs such as the palate, tongue, larynx, fauces, lips, diaphragm, abdominal muscles, back muscles, facial muscles, the feet, legs, buttocks, and in fact every part of our unsuspecting anatomies.

The second class has developed all kinds of fads and fancies, often so ridiculous as to excite our mirth, so ingenious as to promote our astonishment. A collection of these fads and fancies is given on page 51 of this book.

The third class, as might be supposed, is nearer the truth. Books of this class have been written by unprejudiced men and women, both teachers and singers of more or less reputation. They often teach us real facts regarding the voice and its action, and they sometimes give us excellent empirical ideas of real value for the teaching and practice of singing.

It seems strange, however, that no one has as yet written a clear treatise upon the natural laws governing the vocal organs and the organs which assist them in their action, accompanied by a definitely arranged system of teaching based upon cause and effect, which will instruct teacher and pupil how to hear, and how to cure by at least approximately definite means, both inherent and acquired faults in singing. If there is such a book, it has not yet reached my attention.

The ideas and principles which I have endeavoured to present in this book are largely the result of making copious notes during my own experience as singer and teacher, daily, almost hourly, and they have been practically proved by this experience during a period of more than twenty-five years.

I have little patience with many of the antiquated ideas often brought forward as truths long established, many of which are of doubtful origin, nor with much of the so-called "science" of voice masquerading under a cloak of verbosity, nor with the ridiculous tricks which singers are obliged to adopt in certain, and unfortunately too many, studios. On the other hand, I have the utmost respect for the knowledge, both scientific and empirical, which has been handed down, largely by word of mouth, by the great teachers of old. Many of the principles advocated in this book are based partly upon this traditional but true knowledge.

There is only one way to sing: with obedience to natural law. If we disobey the law we must pay the price.

I have purposely adopted a form of writing calculated to make ideas plain, and I have avoided as much as possible the use of technical terms and names. I have also indulged in a certain amount of repetition so as to avoid misunderstanding and incorrect assumption on the part of the reader.

My experience with teachers compels me to believe that there is a real demand for a book which will tell them how to teach and why. Perhaps this is especially true of American teachers and singers. The American mind is not naturally an obedient mind, but an enquiring mind. It is not ready to accept as proof of a fact the mere assertion of that fact. The American pupil is certain to ask "WHY?" at every turn of the road, and the teacher must be ready with the reason, or fail! The teacher should be able, then, to give reasonable and easily understood explanations of the various laws, facts, principles, functions, limitations, etc., with which the singer has to deal, without burdening the pupil's mind with unnecessary detail or scientific language.

I myself studied with many teachers both in the United States and Europe. I continually asked "why," but I seldom got a satisfying answer. Some teachers were patient and tried to explain, but had not the required knowledge to do so. Others flew into a passion, enraged because they knew that they did not know. I learned little from most of them, because it was impossible for me to do things without knowing how and why, and also because I had a very stubborn and unruly voice and throat which took years to conquer. But I did learn that many of the teachers of

singing were guessing nearly all the time, and that few had a
method of teaching based upon real knowledge and law.  Tricks,
"stunts," absurdities of all kinds, were what we bought.  Some
talked science, some preached psychology, some quite frankly
experimented, and learned more from the pupil than the pupil
learned from the teacher.  One teacher told me to "pull in" when
I inhaled, another to "push out."  One, to place my voice at the
back, another at the front.  One told me that the bass voice was
placed more in the head than even the soprano, another that it
was placed entirely in the chest.  One said to form the lips like
a trumpet, another to sing with a smile.  One taught that the
higher tones went back, another that they were placed in the
forehead.  One insisted upon a high larynx, another upon a low
larynx.  One placed the high tones in all pupils with the aid of
the vowel OO, another with EE.  One told me to lean forward
and bow the head, another to press the head and neck backward
against the collar.  One said to "focus" the voice in the upper
front teeth, another to focus in the back part of the hard palate.
One, to "feel" something, another to "think" something.  And
so on endlessly!  There was no idea of natural law or of coördination.  It was all specialization reduced to localization.  Let
the reader think for a moment of the needless waste of time
and money, and what is worse, the mental torture of such an
experience.

### Dangers of Specializing

Much of all this wandering in method and principle, if you
can call it principle, can be explained.

In all branches of learning we have been specialized to death.
Also the spirit of the past two or three decades has largely been
a spirit of getting quick results in every form of endeavour.  Work
is affected by the spirit of the times in which it exists.  Art is no
exception.  So, even in singing, everybody has been seeking the
"short cut" to glory, an emancipation from hard work coupled
with patience, concentration and industry.  It has been the age
of the throat specialist, stomach specialist, nerve specialist, voice
specialist!  The same is true of the business world.  I am not
saying that it is not a necessary condition, but I do say it is a
dangerous condition.  It breeds a knowledge which of necessity
must become one-sided.  In the case of the throat specialist, for
instance, we see, almost daily, errors in treatment which are due
to this one-sided vision.  Many if not most of the affections of the
throat, nose, etc., are not local but systemic in their origin, and

respond far better to treatment based upon systemic cause than to local treatment alone. So, most of the trouble with the singing voice, so far as "vocal production" is concerned, is due to faulty coördination rather than to a local fault.

All this brings up the interesting question of education, the fundamental source of the further development of mankind. Do we need *more* education, or *better* education? Is it wise or beneficial for so many men and women to go to college and become "educated" to the extreme? Is it sensible for so many thousands to study the arts when only a few hundreds possess talent sufficient to insure them a modicum of success for their labor and pains and expense? Is it wise to trust so much to specialization and "division of labor," thereby narrowing more and more the vision which is necessary for complete development?

I believe that any person giving serious thought to the prevailing conditions in general and particular education, must agree that there is an alarming spirit of superficiality existent as a result of modern educational methods. This is not a wholesale condemnation of modern methods, but it is a warning which we must all observe regarding the trend of the system of the day. It is something of a paradox that the more we have specialized the less thorough we have become. We have become, at any rate, one-sided to a degree which is lacking in breadth if not in depth, and therefore impractical because only partly true; although our specialization was developed with the idea of becoming more thorough and practical.

Hand in hand with this specialization and superficiality has grown the desire for luxury and ease. These were never yet the parents of deep learning and thoroughness.

It is interesting in considering the extent to which education has been pushed in reaching all classes and conditions of people, to observe how it has affected these people, and, what is perhaps of equal importance, how it has affected education itself. As we have spread education more and more widely, have we or have we not been obliged to spread it more thinly in spite of our best endeavour? I refer to the supply of competent teachers as well as to the exaction of compulsory education.

There would also seem to be a very great change in the attitude of the young in choosing a profession, notably the profession of singing. How many seek to become good or great singers and artists because of an intense love of the art of expression and a real feeling for the art of the singer, and how many choose the singer's career because of the strong possibility of making large, fat fees?

It is not a far-fetched idea that too much learning can make one mad, and in many cases a very little learning can be too much. How many good working people are ruined in their whole sense of proportion in life, in their very happiness, because of "education" which they cannot mentally digest, and which distorts their view not only of life but of the things which they are trying to do and must do to live.

Again, education, even in the profession of the singer, is too often only a memory of facts, and not the lesson of life and experience deduced from those facts. This is probably the greatest weakness of our present methods. There is too much analysis for the sake of detail. There is too little of the finished product of thought and reason through the reconstruction of ideas.

Thoroughness, then, is paramount, no matter what the task or subject. Analysis is of little value in itself, any more than is technique by itself. In our own subject, it is of small value for a teacher to know through a study of anatomy and physiology all the various parts and individual functions of the vocal organs and breathing organs, unless that knowledge enables him, first, to deduce and understand the natural and coördinate laws which govern these organs, and second, to discover methods of teaching and practice which will help himself and his pupils to induce obedience to these laws.

Each generation bewails the backsliding and decadence of the next. As far back as Tosi and Mancini and others we hear of the degeneration of the art of singing, the loss of all skill, ideal and style. But because of this inherent trait in human nature and our desire to avoid it, we must not be blind to faults which really exist, whether they are the faults of degeneration or of supposed progress. So, just because we fear to fall into the old error and criticise foolishly with wholesale condemnation, that does not mean that we must not criticise at all. Certainly, in most particulars, educational methods and opportunities have improved for the many, and specialization has made discoveries impossible under old conditions. So also intensive methods may accomplish much, but he who looks neither to the right nor left is bound to miss many of the lessons of experience and much of the learning which bears largely upon the very subject he is so assiduously pursuing. So also, especially in the arts, it is not all education as such. Intuition, what in our subject we would call "singing sense," is a large and important factor, the very foundation of nature's gift, and any system of education which interferes with this singing sense is bound to fail.

### Technique and Expression are Inseparable

Science is well-ordered knowledge of facts arranged in sequence, is the technique of knowledge; but ART is ideal, inspirational, intuitive. Therefore I cannot subscribe to the exaggerated concept of art as a presentation of the *real* as we recognize it, but rather of the *ideal* as we imagine it. This brings us to the realization that we must train the imagination and inspiration of the artist in every way possible, but *always* with due regard for proportion, good taste, saneness and nobility of purpose, with love of his mission, as his never-failing guides. For that reason, let not "fools rush in where angels fear to tread!" Art is a noble calling! The artist is a kind of missionary, if he is a real artist at heart. This does not mean that he is unworthy of his hire. But woe betide the singer who works for money alone, yes, for glory alone, for he is sure to fail.

Technique, then, is only a part of the education of the singer, even though an important part. It must go hand in hand with the imagination, the recreative power, the interpretative power, the sense of expression, from the very first. And the more he tries to develop the sense of the ideal, of color and expression, with the ear as the unfailing guide, growing more and more acute with practice and experience, the better and more lasting will be the development of the technique.

There is little use in "reviewing" all the faults of modern singers. We know they are faulty, we want only to try to make them better. But we must not forget that singers have always been faulty. There have always been singers who loved to "yell." There have always been individual successes which seemed to refute every known law. There have always been few good singers and fewer great ones. So a tirade about present-day conditions in comparison with the glorious past is of no use. Let us take the world as we find it. Perhaps if we heard the singers of a century or two ago we should not care for them. We do not know! Our task is with to-day, not yesterday. Our mission is to improve, not to reform. We put ourselves in question if we assume a position as much needed saviors of the art of singing. Such an attitude is ridiculous. We may even never "discover" anything as important as the things already discovered, any more than a physician of the future may discover anything so vital to the cause of medicine and surgery as the circulation of the blood (Harvey).

One of the greatest singers who ever lived has recently passed from us, our dear lamented friend Enrico Caruso, and it is not long since our opera sustained most of the glories of vocal art in as difficult a form as the singers of old, even though that form was different. So why wail about degeneration, when what we want is encouragement, improvement, lack of fear, and honest endeavour!

Singers go in cycles; so do all art, religion, politics, knowledge. You cannot shine all the time. There must be periods for growth and recuperation. Changes in conditions on certain sides of life bring changes on other sides. Let us take up our task as we find it, ready with a strong love of our art to try simply and honestly to "clear the way" a little for those who are to follow.

# CHAPTER II

How Technique is Acquired—The Laryngologist : Separation of
Technique from Expression—Coördination—Empiricism
*versus* "Science"—Laws of the Vocal Organs

In the study of an art like singing it is well first of all to
decide just what we are trying to do.

We are trying to discover, after due study and investigation,
the best method of teaching singing. This is not to be confused
with the best "singing method." The first is a very definite
possibility, one that demands form of expression, just as form
must exist in the expression of anything whatsoever. The second
is more or less of a myth, and at most all we can say of a method
of singing is that it is a natural form of activity, just as is walking,
running, etc.

We are trying, then, to find the best manner of teaching
people to sing, so that they will do so naturally without interference with nature's laws. Part of the object of this book is to
attempt to make these laws and their actions clearly understood.

Singing, although a perfectly natural form of expression, must
be acquired in more or less degree, just as we learn to walk, talk,
etc. This seems to me to be a point too frequently forgotten.
Either the arts are artificial, and pure invention, or else they
are natural gifts of mankind, subject to natural laws first, and
subject to their own laws, second.

This must be true of their technique as well as of their expression. That is to say, the arts originate in the imagination,
which is sister to inspiration, and technique is its handmaiden;
and the two are inseparable. I wish to emphasize this point
strongly, that the technique of an art is part of and dependent
upon the art itself, that it is a child of that art and not the creator
of it. It is not a separate science nor even a separate art. Imagination then, as well as will-power, enters intimately into the matter
of both technique and expression.

Let me say again that the technique of any art is dependent
upon the art itself, that there is no such thing as developing a
wonderful technique and then attaching it ready-made to the art.
We find, then, that a method of procedure in teaching which deals

with the mere creation of tone as a mechanical, unimaginative act must fail, because we are attempting the impossible.

Imagination enters even into the singing of scales and exercises. It is perfectly senseless to try to separate even our practice from our real, artistic, creative endeavour, for the two must go together, and one will work directly on the other. Any machine-like method, then, is impossible and senseless. Or rather we might say we are working with a two-part machine, the one flesh and blood, the other mental and imaginative, both together limitless in their variety of combinations, impulses and creations, but separated, perfectly useless. So, the idea of tone creation by means of local effort which limits physiological action, the ideal being a certain machine-like perfection without expression, color, or meaning, is thoroughly impossible, because when we "will" to make a sound we must of necessity have a concept of that sound, which is immediately a command for expression.

Every emotion, every act of the imagination, every uttered thought, even every attempt to sing, when put into words, or tone, or both, instantly colors the tone and the word formed in the tone. The same is true if we merely sing a scale.

Another thing! The technique of the singer or dancer or painter or pianist is good for nothing directly except singing, dancing, painting or piano-playing, and these techniques grow with the imagination of the performer, as well as by physical practice. They are part and parcel of his art. Therefore there is no such thing as working for years for a mere technique, and then attaching it ready-made to the art it is supposed to fit. That is the idea of the local-effort school, mistakenly called by many the scientific school, and it is absolutely false. I mean that the idea of a purely mechanical formation and emission of tone, everything put in its exact place according to "science," locally—the nose, ribs, tongue, palate, larynx, diaphragm, back, lips, etc.— and then applying thought, emotion or imagination afterward, is perfectly ridiculous. So the local-effort school is false because it attempts to divorce two things which cannot be parted and live.

Are we justified, therefore, in going to the other extreme and accepting the dictum that all technique is acquired merely by singing with more or less expression until we can accomplish all of the gradations of tone in all its phases? Hardly, although this would doubtless be preferable to the other, because at least we should cultivate spontaneity in some degree. It seems to me that there is a strong trend in this direction, and we read many assertions that the old masters taught in this fashion of a sort of general criticism of results, without any very clear manner of telling how to get them. This we might call the experimental method, a method of urging the pupil to try to sing tones in any and every way his imagination led him, the teacher's mission being to tell him when it "sounded well." This would doubtless be safer than the local-effort method, which goes directly against nature's laws of coördination and spontaneity of expression. So the books of those who have investigated the methods of past generations have too often resulted in negation rather than in proclamation of definite principles. We read endless assertions that the old masters taught nothing definite, that they used some forgotten ideas of empiricism, suggestion, and imitation; and with this denial of everything concrete, we are left in the air with nothing to take hold of.

We have to contend, if we accept the above, with all kinds of half-truths, fads, fancies, tricks, which have ruined voices, not to speak of lives and careers, and which have put the profession of the teacher of singing in disrepute all over the world. We hear little about the charlatan in the world of the piano or violin teacher, for the simple reason that they are dealing with visible action. The teacher of singing deals with the half-visible, the half-unseen.

I am certain if the teacher of violin or piano should tell his pupil to chase an imaginary dove around the room, to make the "foolish face" so as to "relax," or to make the letter S with his arms, or to think of his biceps when moving his thumbs, the pupil would think him crazy and seek another teacher. Yet the uncertainty of how to approach the dreaded question of "method" in voice training has filled both teacher and pupil with so much doubt, that the one has been willing to resort to anything, no matter how weird or queer, and the other has been willing to accept it, often in the last throes of despair. If all the teachers who indulge in these queer practices were really charlatans, we should have an obvious method of dealing with them. But the greatest difficulty is the fact that most of them are really honest, sincere, hardworking men and women simply laboring under delusions, or fighting against an ignorance which makes them all the more dangerous. Many of the books on singing are as dangerous as the teachers, perhaps more so, for they pass on erroneous ideas as truths, and we all know the power of the printed page. Ideas and assertions are all very well and often interesting, but the crying need is knowledge, accepted knowledge, put into concrete form understandable by all, so that we may finally build up a standardised method of teaching, even if we cannot now or ever standardise tone.　And certainly we should never desire to do the latter, even if it were possible, which it is not.

Many of the questions argued about in books have long since been settled and accepted by men who are authorities.　No matter how long or strong the argument, we shall never be able to accept a method of breathing different from the one used by man since his possession of his present physical form.　Yet even this is still being written about and argued.

## The Laryngologist : Separation of Technique from Expression

As for the vocal organs themselves and their anatomy, with all the theories advanced regarding their separate and allied actions, it seems to me that the teacher of singing has already been burdened with too much science, which is too often only pseudo-science, when it is not merely and palpably guess-work. The laryngologist proclaims a desire to reclaim a degenerate vocal art by means of teachers who are experienced and learned laryngologists acting as "voice-placers," while other teachers, musicians, coaches, etc., will train the singer in the style and interpretation which every artist must acquire.　His argument is that the laryngologist alone should teach the technique of the singer, because he alone understands the physiology and anatomy and functions of the voice organs, can therefore avoid false action, and remedy the same when it has occurred.　By the same argument, the dancing master should understand the anatomy of the legs in order to be a safe teacher of the terpsichorean art, and the violinist should study first with one who understands the anatomy and physiology of the hand and arm, and then in some marvelous fashion attach this technique ready made to his art of expression, which, as we have seen above, cannot be done.　The truth is, we have had too many throat doctors teaching singing, too many extreme ideas and theories given to the pupil of singing, most of which sound well, or (what is even more dangerous) look well in print.

Would any serious minded violinist or pianist study the mere action of fingers and arms with one teacher, and then seek another from whom to learn style and interpretation?　I grant that the singer has need of an accompanist or coach or teacher of style; so has the violinist; but no one can make me believe that the best coach for the singer is one who knows nothing of the singer's technique, for he is likely to demand the impossible and limit the possible, or ruin the singer's real singing style, which after all is very different from other branches of music, or it would not be singing. And on the other hand I do not believe that the laryngologist who is not an excellent and experienced singer and musician can be a great or even competent vocal teacher or "voice specialist."

## Coördination

The truth is, that singing is dependent upon simple laws of coördination which must be obeyed. But natural, coördinate bodily actions are not induced naturally, freely and safely by overattention muscularly to any one locality, except possibly in extreme cases of faulty action, generally acquired, and accompanied by chronic fatigue. Even then local effort produces doubtful results. In further refutation of the argument in question, it is rather interesting to take notice of the past, the past recently referred to by one writer as the "non-progressive empiricism of the old Italian school of Bel Canto."

The greatest teachers of the past were singers and musicians who knew by *hearing*, not by *observation* alone, what beautiful tone and perfect expression were. That was the rock upon which they built their knowledge. The statement that they had no definite knowledge is in reality without foundation. And some of their knowledge was scientific. Science is knowledge gained by systematic observation, experiment and reasoning; also, knowledge coördinated and arranged. The former is true of the old school, and perhaps even the latter. Mancini certainly tells us some very definite things about his own observation and teaching; so does Tosi, so do others. Mancini particularly tells us that the fauces must point forward, and calls attention to the fact that "modern singers" (that is, singers of the latter half of the eighteenth century) were trying to get more power by stretching or tensing the fauces, to the detriment of their voices, which one assertion tells us as plainly as possible that he believed in singing with freely active fauces, which means freely active palate, at least without willful tension applied locally.

## Empiricism *versus* "Science"

One writer tells us, in summing up his investigations, that the singer is only hampered by scientific teaching, that the only true method is the purely empirical, and that all the singer need do to acquire a good technique is to sing plenty of good music. It will be seen, I think, that both views are untenable, that both laryngologist and empiricist are in error. The one proclaims that only the scientific teacher can succeed, and the other that the singer need not study at all for technique, but simply acquires it as he goes singing on his joyful way. This writer states specifically that the singer has no need of exercises to develop his voice, that in this respect he is freed from the burden of work and exacting practice which the violinist or pianist must endure. Of the two, he is, in my opinion, nearer the truth, and as a singer I would certainly rather take my chances with the really spontaneous system advocated by him, if one can call it a system, than place myself at the mercy of the laryngologist, followed by study with a coach.

The truth lies somewhere between the two opinions. Every art demands a technique, every art has its scientific side, every art has its side of expression. That the latter is paramount every one will agree, and it is to that end that we study. Technique by itself is nearly worthless, expression without technique is impossible; but an overdose of "science" will never give the first, which makes the second possible.

There is one way and one alone to teach singing, and that is by singing. The less we are obliged to take notice of local actions or results, the better off we are. But that does not mean that we must not take any notice of them at all. As singing is a physical act, it must be obedient to bodily physical laws, which are always laws of coördination.

## Laws of the Vocal Organs

The laws of the voice organs are few and simple. They divide themselves into three "families" of action, (1) the swallowing or eating acts, (2) the speech and singing acts, and (3) the respiration acts. The first two are the two "families of action" most varied and interesting.

The work of the teacher of singing divides itself naturally into two branches of endeavour, the training of the novice to become a real singer, and the restoring of injured voices. The object of this very simple and informal work is to try to tell the reader how I believe the teacher can best meet these two tasks, and in fairness to the reader let me say now in the plainest terms, that if he is seeking a book on anatomy, this is not the book for him.

To my mind a source of great confusion and actual misunderstanding for many years has been the consideration of the voice as some material thing possessed of tangible shape and form which can be "placed" here or there in various parts of our mouths, faces, or bodies. Voice is not material in the sense of a movable thing. Voice is sound, and is therefore subject to the laws of vibration and sound. We read continually of "pulling the voice back into the throat," of "lifting" the voice, of "placing" the voice, etc. In reality we do none of these things. Sound as such will "go" in all directions, unless there is some obstruction to the vibrations and sound-waves of which sound is made. That is to say, if you alter the position of the voice organs so that certain cavities are altered in their shape or partly cut off from the other cavities, you limit the "going" of the sound which we call voice. Or, in other words, you change the character of resonance of the voice and therefore the voice itself, because you have by a physical act limited or prevented the use of certain resonance cavities, limited the "going" of the vibrations.

Again, if you change the position of the tongue in certain ways, you alter the mouth cavity and change the resonance of the voice, obtaining a variety of vowels and consonants exactly in proportion to the altering of the tongue position. If you pull the tongue back into the pharynx, you cause the voice to sound hollow, or guttural, or "dark," and you are told that you have drawn the voice far back into the throat, whereas you have done nothing of the kind. You have simply interfered with the correct tongue action or position, or both, with the result that the voice assumes the color allied to the cavities in which you have allowed it to be resonated. But you have not placed the voice in any way. You have simply interfered with correct physical action.

So, voice is not a thing to be handled or controlled in the sense of putting it somewhere, somehow, but it is vibration causing sound-waves, made into what we call voice by command of the will, stimulated by the imagination, working through and with the vocal organs in obedience to perfectly natural, understandable physical laws. This attitude toward the subject is of the utmost importance, otherwise the following pages will be of no value. Therefore let us understand our point of view before we go any further. You cannot "pull" the voice far back into the throat, because you have nothing to pull it with. It is not a "pullable" quantity. You cannot in reality sing "back," or "front," or "middle," you cannot "place" your voice anywhere, your voice is not a "stream of vocalized breath" to be squirted this way or that as fancy or your teacher dictates, you cannot "think" it somewhere or anywhere, and, most important of all, it will behave itself if you leave it alone. Of course, that is the very thing which is so difficult to do.

It may be seen from such examples that studio terminology and vocal parlance have led to the use of expressions which are not in reality true to fact, which are confusing and actually misleading.

We find the same curious trend in suggestions given to pupils with the hope or intention of persuading certain improvements in physiological action. We read countless suggestions to "relax" until the voice is produced with the vocal organs in a state of complete relaxation,—a manifest impossibility, for we do nothing, *physically*, with complete relaxation, except die!

We also read many advices to have the mental suggestion of "being tired" for this same relaxation. Again a completely false idea and suggestion, for no correct coördinate physical act can be excited and accomplished by means of "that tired feeling."

Relaxation is urged with the mistaken idea of preventing false tension, without anything being given to insure correct action.

So we must realize that correct singing is not directly the result of relaxation, but of correct physical action.

It is again the separation of the technique from the art of expression. The question of relaxation is one of the most maddening to deal with, because in correct singing, as in other acts, we are not in reality relaxed, but in a state of "free activity," unhampered by any interference with nature's laws. This is not relaxation, it is correct action, which is something very different.

# CHAPTER III

## The Primes of Speech and Tone—Language—Breath

As a matter of fact, we can make no singing sound without pronouncing some vowel. The primary vowel, as we shall show later, is AH. We shall show that AH contains and forms complete tone, in pitch (both relative and individual) and in resonance. We might say that the vocal organs in forming this vowel are in a position nearest to their normal "at rest" position. From this vowel we progress through all the other vowels by actions of the voice organs which follow simple, definite, and easily understood laws of progressive action. By other acts of the vocal organs we form the consonants. But in and during these acts we must take cognizance of that resonance so much talked about, for it is changes in the resonance of the voice which allow speech forms to be made; and again, it is other changes in the resonances which cause or perfect tonal changes such as pitch, volume, color, quality, etc. That these two series of changes and readjustments working together, or only too often fighting each other so that they cannot work together, give the singer his chief difficulties, we all know; as we shall see later, they explain very simply why it is difficult to pronounce words on high notes, and also why some words are more difficult to sing than others, either on high or low notes.

This fact, and the easily confused acts of singing and swallowing, are really the sources of most of our difficulties; the terminology used in the teaching of singing for many generations partly proving this fact.

I have read in several books that singers who *sing in their throats* (that is, with constricted internal or external muscles of the throat) cannot pronounce words which will be understandable. Yet we have all heard many singers in vaudeville, concert and opera, who, in spite of a throaty production which makes one ache in sympathy, cause us to hear and understand every syllable they utter, while the tone-quality is execrable.

It seems to me, then, that the voice may be regarded as a musical instrument which has for its primary and instrumentally characteristic sound the vowel AH, and that we have the power to add to this instrumental tone all the speech sounds which exist in any tongue. Therefore, the singing voice would seem to follow the inherent law of nature, in every way, that everything human is dual in action.

## Language

Far too much has been made out of the difference in the "singing value" of the various languages. As a matter of fact, Italian is phonetically the purest and simplest tongue now spoken, its phonetic differences being fewer and clearer than those of other languages. As a purely instrumental medium, a tonal medium, I would place Italian first of all tongues. As a medium for expression I would do no such thing, for it would depend upon what we are singing. Languages grow from racial characteristics and tendencies, they suit the psychology of the race to which they belong, and therefore best express the sentiments of that race. Perhaps this affords the chief difficulty in the translation of opera, songs, etc. At any rate, it is simply a question of using more or fewer forms, more or fewer vowels and consonants, or (what is nearer the truth) more or fewer modifications of certain primes existent in all speech. We shall see in a later chapter, when the laws of the voice organs are understood and their progressive actions explained, that it is perfectly possible to sing practically as well in one language as another. I am speaking now of what are called the Aryan tongues.

Each language, however, presents individual difficulties, because of certain predominant and inherent tendencies. For instance, we have the nasal tendency of the French, the guttural tendency of the German, the "open" sound of the Italian, the flat sound in "man," "can," etc., and the dull "AH" in English, etc., etc. Combinations of consonants also present difficulties in certain languages, often confusing the operation of the vocal tonal law. Climate and environment also affect language and pronunciation.

## Breath

More nonsense has been written about breathing, "breath pressure," "singing on the breath," "singing straight from the diaphragm," "abdominal breathing," "muscular breathing," "psychological breathing," "breath impetus," "division and distribution of breath," "holding back the breath," etc., etc., than could possibly be contained in any book of sane dimensions.

The latest proclamation is that singing makes breathing, but breathing does not make singing; mere nonsense, for they both make each other. Breath helps make the voice go, and using the voice makes us use the breath. In singing, breath and breath-control are of self-evident importance, and if breath-supply, or flow of breath, or breath-pressure, or whatever you please to call it, is related to voice and vocal action, then we can assume, again by commonsense reasoning, that there will be a normal breath effort or supply for a normal tone, i.e., for a tone of medium pitch and volume. By the same reasoning, then, there will be a sub-normal breath effort or supply for a tone of lower pitch and lower volume, and an acute normal, if we may use such a term, for a tone of high pitch and greater volume. I use volume here in the sense of loudness. Any two of these may be combined, i.e., we may have a tone of low pitch and large volume, or one of medium pitch and small volume, or a tone of high pitch and large or small volume, etc. Therefore there must be a law governing the intensity of the breath effort as related to pitch and volume. That law as I see it is as follows: The intensity of the breath effort[1] is commensurate with the tone in pitch and volume.

This means that it takes more breath effort to sing high than it does to sing low, more breath effort to sing loud than soft. Any singer knows that this is so. The mere fact that common sense would dictate economy of breath does not change the law. In relation to this fact, we know that another form of energy is expended in singing, namely, muscular energy, no matter how much we may dislike to mention it. That is, the vocal cords and their surrounding muscles, the muscles which control breathing, and even other muscles in the body, are using up vital force and energy.

The expenditure of this vital force increases with pitch and volume, which explains why we cannot sing very loudly or very high pitches for any great length of time, although some singers come very near doing so.

So when we read all the strange instructions about "holding back the breath" (which we cannot do and do not need to do), about "driving the breath with the diaphragm" (which we also cannot do in the purely natural, balanced act of respiration), and all the other fads about breath-control, we can simply remember this natural and self-evident law, realizing that we must again turn to nature to find some way of study which will aid us in not interfering with her laws. I remember a teacher who expounded to me at great length why it took more breath, actually more air, to sing *piano* than to sing *forte;* which of course is ridiculous, as is proved by our law.

[1]By breath effort is meant not only the amount of air, but actual muscular energy.

As a matter of fact, the rapidity of vibration of the cords causes the differences in pitch, the extent or width of the swing of the cords causes primary volume of tone, the mission of the breath being dual, first to help cause vibration, and second to supply "material" for vibration. It is still possible that we may find a nerve control which also causes the cords to vibrate, regulating both pitch and volume by direct control.

We are also told that singers should breathe with their legs, that they form or create a vacuum in the lungs, that the larynx must resist the great force of the breath driven upwards, and other things which are astounding in an age which boasts of rather general knowledge of the laws of physics and physiology.

# CHAPTER IV

## Resonance—Actions of the Vocal Organs—Pronunciation

Probably not even the question of breath has caused more dire confusion and uncertainty, not to speak of faulty emission of voice, than this comparatively new bugaboo, RESONANCE! Yet resonance is a simple and easily understood phenomenon.

The weak, simple, almost "toneless tone" sent up by the vocal cords, is communicated to all the cavities which it can reach, and by a sort of echoing or resounding process is changed into musical vocal tone, or speech tone.

If we examine the vocal organs as a complete organism, we find that, if we limit our vision to the regions above the vocal cords (that is, from the larynx upwards), we can liken them to a kind of two-part trumpet. The throat is the tube, branching at the pharynx into two "horns," the mouth and the head. The vocal cords are the "vibrator," the throat is the tube, the mouth is the first resonator, the head and nasal cavities are the second resonator. We find again that we can change the shape and therefore the value of the first resonator at will, and that while we cannot really change the shape of the upper resonator, which is fixed, we *can* change the extent to which we use it, by natural means. That is, we can change the proportion of one resonator to the other, and we can definitely change the shape of the first or mouth resonator. We might say that we "stop" or modify either or both of these resonators to the degree in which we use them individually, or in their proportion to each other. (The idea of the two-part trumpet is from my very dear and lamented friend Dr. H. H. Curtis, who taught us much about the resonances of the voice.)

By "stopping" the resonance of the mouth, for instance, we not only alter the "tone," but we make certain speech forms. For instance, starting with the vowel AH, the nearest "at rest" position, by raising the tongue forward a certain degree we sound the vowel Ā, and by increasing the raising of the tongue to a certain higher degree we obtain the vowel E (English). That is, we "stop" the resonance of the mouth enough to change the AH into Ā or E, or, by raising the tongue, we lessen the size and change the shape of the resonator of the mouth, so that the sound of AH is changed into Ā or E. Similarly, we change the mouth resonator for purposes of speech, thus "stopping" or changing the resonance, not only with the tongue, but with the palate, fauces, uvula, lips. We can alter or "stop" the resonance of the tube of the throat by means of the epiglottis, which can fold up against the tongue, or fold down over the larynx, and by pulling back the tongue, and by raising or lowering the larynx, etc. Again, by means of the palate, uvula and fauces, we may alter the use of the resonance of the head and nasal cavities in such fashion as to make possible an endless number of proportions or combinations with the resonance of the mouth, or we may cut off the mouth resonance nearly completely.

In like fashion we can cut off the nasal and head resonance nearly completely, or "stop" it nearly completely, by means of the palate, etc. It is an established fact that as the speech changes occur in resonation, sympathetic changes occur in the action of the cords, which may be "causation" differences, or reflex differences caused by the speech changes in the use of the resonators, what are termed "reactions."

From this view of the resonators 1 and 2, mouth and head, as a two-part trumpet, we get an idea of the endless number of possible changes in color or resonance or quality or pitch or volume in the human voice. We would naturally assume that, except for very rare sounds, we should never reach the actual cutting off of one resonator from the other, and therefore the two resonators are sounding practically all the time during the singing act, and we can easily discover what would be the result if we do cut off one from the other. But the main fact is that the two resonators are being used in varying proportion to each other all the time during the singing act. We have a third resonator, the chest, and possibly the whole body. But certainly the latter is beyond our powers of analysis as a resonator. But we who have sung, all have felt, very distinctly, the resounding and vibrating of the chest. We might say that the chest not only contains the "bellows" or lungs with which we breathe, and with which we supply needed air to the cords, but it is a resonator as well, a resonator below the cords or vibrator, in the opposite direction from the flow of the air upwards, and therefore an "indirect" resonator. Now all these resonators are connected, by means of the continuation of the TUBE of our two-part trumpet. We can at will use more of one than of the other two. As these resonators are connected, we can and do use all three of them at the same time, and all the time. That is, every tone has chest resonance, mouth, and head resonance, and these resonances alter their proportion to each other for purposes of pitch, color, quality and volume. Then there must be a law applicable to this change or series of changes. If we accept again the simile of the trumpet, with the chest as a kind of sounding-board, then we can say, always for practical purposes, that each tone of the singing voice has chest, mouth and head resonance, and that these three resonances change their ratio to each other for each tone. If we accept this view, and I cannot see how we can accept anything else, we eliminate an ancient bugbear for all time—the really absurd doctrine of registers. There is one register of the human voice, and only one, but there are three distinct qualities, the chest quality, the mouth quality, the head quality, and these qualities are simply due to resonation in the three districts above mentioned.

The chest resonance gives depth and organ-like *quality;* the mouth gives the *"yell"* of the voice, the "stentorian" *quality,* brilliant, piercing, primary, the very core of the voice; the head gives the sonority, the sweetness, the softness, the quality that reduces the "yell" of the mouth's brilliancy and the depth and darkness of the chest into real musical, sympathetic, "human" tone. But it cannot be too much emphasized that the really perfect tone, unlimited in expression, demands all three resonances to attain its perfection, no matter how predominant one may be, or how weak another.

As I said above, if these things are true, then there must be a law of action, a law that will establish some coherence in the relative action of these three resonances and of their proportion to each other. As the pitch ascends, the chest resonance grows less, the mouth resonance increases and the head resonance increases in higher ratio than the mouth. But the mouth remains always the "centre of effort," the centre of action, the core of the voice, the real pronouncing organ, and the central resonator, the actual former of the voice, but dependent upon its assisting resonators, the chest and the head. Without them, musically, it is nothing. This is what makes man different from and above the animal. It makes language possible, and through the development of language through countless ages, singing.

If then we accept the fact that every tone possesses resonances of all three resonators, we must deny the existence of registers in the voice, unless we allow each interval of a semitone to constitute a new register. And if we allow that, we must allow more, for we can sound intervals of less than a semitone, so that the number of registers would be without limit, and no possible good could be gained by any such argument. It is far simpler and more sensible to deny the existence of registers, which, as proved above, originated in the recognition of the three predominant qualities caused by the three principle resonators.

One of the laws of acoustics is that two sounds of different pitch cannot be resonated in the same resonator with equal result. As the voice is not provided with many separate resonators tuned to each separate pitch, the existing resonators are simply used in varied proportion to each other, thereby providing a new and perfectly tuned resonator for each and every tone of the voice. This is not only a matter of pitch, but of quality and volume and speech.

Perhaps it will now be seen that we do not really "place" the voice "forwards" or "back" or "up" or "down" or *any*-"where." We sing *every*-"where" according to the kind of tone we want to make, the kind of sentiment or emotion we wish to express. The attempt to sing in one "place" is simply imposing a limit upon color and expression.

### Actions of the Vocal Organs

The actions of the vocal organs, that is, those organs closely allied with pronunciation, pitch, quality, volume, color, etc., are also closely allied with what we call resonance in the human voice, and they are also concerned with the act of eating and swallowing, and the act of respiration.

Omitting their respiratory activity for the moment, let us consider them in a general way in regard to their activities for speech or singing and for eating and swallowing.

These activities resolve themselves into two "families of action," the coördinations for the various forms of speech and tone, and the various coördinations for eating and swallowing.

Yet we read and hear countless instructions, suggestions and "urges" toward local and separate muscular action and control, without the least regard to the coördinate laws governing these organs and their actions.

Pupils are taught to locally flatten the tongue, to push it towards the teeth, to curl it backwards, even to "hump" it up at the back part; to "groove" it, to "distribute" it sideways, to relax the jaw, to pull the jaw backwards, to locally raise the palate, to raise or lower the larynx, to trumpet the lips, to exaggerate the smiling position, etc., etc., without the least regard to the fact that there is sympathetic action governing the various voice organs, and in absolute ignorance of the laws that govern the actions of these organs.

When we swallow, the larynx rises, the epiglottis folds down over the larynx to prevent the passage of food into the windpipe, also the arytenoids push forward for the same purpose, the tongue pulls back to throw the food down the throat, and the palate rises upwards and backwards against the back wall of the throat to prevent food and drink from going into the nasal passages. It is all a coördinate action, perfectly natural, part of the natural functions of these organs. When we prevent this action by talking, laughing, etc., during the swallowing act, we interfere with the coördination of these swallowing acts of the voice organs, and we choke.

The singing and speech act is exactly opposite to the swallowing act. The larynx remains in its natural position, gradually turning backwards and downwards at its rear, as the pitch ascends, the tongue plunges upwards and forwards, the glottis closes as the cords approximate by means of the revolution of the arytenoids, and their backward pull, the epiglottis folds up against the tongue in various degrees of nearness; the palate moves forwards, never backwards, rising slightly with the pitch; the fauces "point forward" at their upper extremities, gradually approximating as the pitch ascends, and the uvula rises until it has entirely or nearly entirely disappeared. This is also a perfectly natural coördinate action. When these two natural series of acts get mixed up or confused, we either choke in eating, or we "swallow" our tones during singing and speech, or some other faulty characteristic appears in our singing. As these organs are very sensitive, as the palate in particular is made of erective tissue easily excited, and is very sensitive even to sound and air, and as the whole organism is surrounded by and contains almost countless nerves, there is small wonder that things can go wrong very easily. In other words, we interfere with the natural functions of these organs, or rather they are so closely allied that they easily interfere with each other, and therein lies the chief difficulty of the singer.

We know that if we locally exaggerate the action of one organ or one part of a coördination we interfere with that coördination of which the action of that organ is a part. It is manifestly impossible to indulge in any of the local acts mentioned above exactly according to a general coördination, and in exact proportion to the result sought. Unfortunately, we *can* control or move many of the sound-producing organs locally. The singer obeys the "local" instructions, seems to obtain a benefit thereby, but in the near future finds that he has only exchanged one fault for another, or that the original fault may be even worse than it was.

If the action of the voice organs in singing follows a certain trend, there must be a law. We may frame this law in two fashions:

(1) In general, the action of the vocal organs in singing is exactly opposite to their action in swallowing.

(2) In general, the action of the vocal organs in singing is upwards and forwards, except the larynx, which revolves on its own axis, descending at the back in proportion to pitch. The lips demand special attention. (These laws will be explained more fully in the second part of this book.)

It will be seen from the above that the action of the vocal organs is coördinate, that is, they act in relation to, and in a manner dependent upon, each other. They perform functions for purposes of pitch, changes in resonance, quality, volume, and speech or pronunciation. It is therefore easy to imagine how much harm can be done by "local effort," trying to hold the tongue flat, raising the palate, widening the fauces, raising or lowering the larynx. The actions of the vocal organs must be in harmony with each other, they should obey their natural laws, and again, we must find some way or method of teaching which will enable the pupil to learn how to sing without interfering with these natural coördinate acts. For it would be manifestly impossible to fasten one's attention upon the tongue, for instance, to flatten that member, and yet flatten it exactly in proportion to the actions of the other vocal organs. This is the best and clearest argument against local control.

It will be seen, then, that singing does not differ from all the other natural functions or acts or abilities of man. All must be acquired by long and patient endeavour, dependent upon the natural adaptability of the individual. So we say a man or woman has a natural talent for a certain art, because he or she becomes adept in that art with less endeavour than most other persons. This does not mean that we need lose valuable time in learning. We learn to walk and talk slowly and painfully from infancy, with many a bump and fall in the former, and with many a foolish incoherency in the latter. It is not all physical, it is not all psychological.

It is mental, imaginative, wilful, technical, imitative! It is again coördination, and we are not in any true measure successful except after years of trying. But in singing we can at least save time and eliminate much of the mere "experimental," because of our advance in years and knowledge, reason and judgment. Therefore, we can acquire the technique of singing in less time than even speech, because we are already experienced in a large degree with speech forms and their accompanying technique. We are more or less experienced in expression also, in imagination, will-power, and perhaps, above all, in *concentration*. But we must always keep in mind the fact that we are cultivating natural functions, that we are simply developing something already there, and not "learning" an unnatural science. And so we must learn to sing by means of some system which will allow and persuade nature to behave herself, or rather in such a manner as not to put anything in the way of nature. And again, by developing the real "impulse to sing," by allowing our imaginations to grow and increase in scope and originality, we shall give new impulse and development to those functions which we call technical as well as to the organs which perform the functions.

There must be some definite guide to help us on our way, and we find that the best guide is the ear, what we might call the court of ultimate resort. But the eye can also help us, and so we have what we might call "visible" faults in singing, and "hearable" faults. If we are not careful we shall find that over-attention to the former will tempt us unduly to local effort. The ear, then, is the chief guide for singing, just as the eye is for painting. On the other hand, to say that we must never use local effort would be absurd, for it can be of great assistance if used correctly, but it cannot and must not be the real basis of teaching or learning.

Above all we must remember that technique is simply the result of perfect and habitual obedience to the natural laws which govern the vocal organs, plus the imagination which commands the act.

The argument may be advanced that if this is so, why not accept the dictum that we need simply keep on singing plenty of good music until we obtain the skill we seek. Simply because we must creep before we can walk or run!

By the singing of scales we limit the extent and demands of our imagination, we ask less of the vocal organs. We sing, as it were, along the normal tonal line, on fundamental vowel and tone, before attempting the more enlightened forms of expression. We cultivate the use of our instrument, *as* an instrument, to obtain a real control over it, exactly as does the violinist or pianist, the only difference being that the singer and his instrument are one. I do not believe this makes the matter more difficult, but on the contrary less difficult. And I certainly do not believe in confining the singer to years of "five-finger" exercises until he has become a kind of vocal gymnast. There is reason and common sense in all things. So, the teacher must seek out the individual qualities of his pupil, and while all must of necessity obey the same laws, they will not all take the same time or exactly the same means to learn that obedience.

When we acknowledge the need of common sense in teaching singing, and see that we are dealing with natural laws, we can see plainly the fallacy in the methods that are only too prevalent, and have always been too prevalent.

I not only believe that we seldom accomplish real good by telling singers to "do" certain *local* things, but I believe that we harm them by so doing, and retard their progress, except in the instances taken up in the second part of this book. For instance, do not tell a singer to open his throat, because he cannot do so, he does not know where to begin, and he will always only partly succeed and will incur throat tension by trying. By the same token, do not tell a singer to flatten his tongue, or push it forward, or to raise or lower his palate, or to lower his larynx. The mere attempt to do so will bring about another fault worse in many cases than the fault he is trying to correct. All of these local faults in coördination can be corrected in other ways much safer and more true to nature, as we shall see.

When we review the sections regarding breathing and the actions of the vocal organs, when we put the two parts of the machine together, as it were, we find that the law of the breath in relation to tone, and the laws of the action of the voice organs, combined, form a new law.

For as the intensity of the breath effort is commensurate with the tone in pitch and volume, and as the action of the vocal organs is generally upwards and forwards in proportion to pitch and volume, so the action of the voice organs is proportionate to the intensity of the breath effort. Again it is coördination, beginning with the first instant of the act of inhaling, and finishing with the last instant of "breath-support."

We shall see in Part II how the act of inhaling "prepares us to sing," by relaxing and freeing the entire vocal apparatus, putting it into a state of free activity, ready for any necessary act.

We see then that the vocal pipe goes through changes exactly in proportion to the pitch and volume of the tone; that these changes follow definite laws, and that they are accompanied and partly caused by the changes in the breath effort, which are in their turn subject to their own law.

## Pronunciation

Pronunciation is of the utmost importance in singing as in speech.

A beautiful speaking voice and perfect pronunciation are as rare as is the perfect singer.

The key to perfect pronunciation is the formation of perfectly pure and simple vowels, and perfectly clear cut and "quick," un-obstructed consonants. It is amazing how the mere attempt to pronounce a phrase or word clearly and correctly in speech will overcome difficulties in singing, such as pronouncing certain words on high notes. We all know the story of Jenny Lind about her hours of practice to sing the word "zersplittre" on high B flat. She pronounced it over and over again until she could *pronounce* the word so perfectly and easily that she *sang* it just as easily in the end.

The use of the mouth in singing, as the mouth is our chief "pronouncer," must concern our art most vitally. If the vocal organs and therefore the organs of "pronouncing" obey certain laws in proportion to tone, and as the pronouncing organs must go through certain changes for the formation of words, working on a principle of "stopped" resonances (as we have seen), how then can these two functions take place at the same time without interference? They do not do so. Let us take some simple ex-amples. Supposing we sing the vowel AH, the prime of both tone and speech, from our lowest note to our highest. We shall notice at once that no matter how perfectly we sing, the vowel goes through certain changes or modifications. These modifica-tions will not be very "hearable" to us at first until they reach the higher notes. But we shall find after some attention and keen listening that one note in this range sounds a more perfect AH than any other. That is, we shall find that some note in the medium "normal" of the vocal range sounds what we call a per-fect AH, and that the notes below it and above it sound a slightly different AH. Sing other vowels in the same "test," and the same result will be noticed. Now try another "test." Sing any sentence (say five or six words) upon one note in the lower range, then the same words upon a tone in the middle range, and again the same words upon a tone almost as high as you can sing. You will find that it is much easier to sing the words at the "middle" pitch than upon either of the others, but you will find especial difficulty in singing the words at the high pitch. Why? Because the laws of pronunciation and the laws of tone are not the same. Because (as we shall see in Part II) the laws for tone (that is, pitch, volume, color, etc.) are fixed, and the resonators must exactly follow these laws. But the laws for speech forms, also radical in their demands, are frequently antagonistic to pitch and even color, and must give way to them. In other words, we may *modify a vowel sound* without losing its character, but *pitch* is unyielding. So we obtain the principle of vowel modification, and we shall formulate a law concerning it in the second part of this book. As the consonants are short and unsustained, we can easily conquer such difficulties as they present.

The main thing is, to know *why* it is difficult to sing certain words on high tones; if we know *why*, we can find out *how* to solve the difficulty.

One of the greatest difficulties for English and American singers in pronunciation is due to the "vanish" of certain vowels in their language. The O in English finishes with the vanish OO. We say O-OO.

The Ā vanishes with E, the I vanishes with E, and is in reality made up of AH and E. These vanishes when prolonged give a "provincial" touch to the pronunciation, and if at all exaggerated become very disagreeable. So also, certain false pronunciations are very prevalent, such as "sheall" for "shall," due to a false concept of the consonant "h." Also we hear "rejeoice," for "rejoice," because of a false concept of the consonant "j." The Italian has the advantage in this matter of pure and single sounds, for the "vanish" does not exist in his tongue.

The modification of the vowels, and the perfect action of the vocal organs for tone, does not injure or make indistinct our pronunciation, or harm our enunciation and emission. On the contrary, the obedience to the natural laws of singing, which causes the slight modification, is alone possible if we accept this doctrine, and the result will be far more natural and spontaneous and true to laws of pronunciation than if we force the vowels to sound in their "medium-normal" form. It is perhaps the latter forcing which causes many singers to sing out of tune on their higher notes. It also explains how many vaudeville singers can let us hear and understand every syllable of every word, and yet produce evil sounding and vicious tones.

Perhaps the greatest change in "vocal method" from the old doctrines is in the use of the lips. The old idea was to sing with the lips shaped like a slight smile. Why? Because, after all, it was found to be the natural shape of the lips for nearly all the speech sounds, and the best for tone, because it is allied closely to the natural actions of the tongue and other vocal organs. Of recent years the opposite shape has been advised by many if not most teachers. Singers have wanted dark, round, "big" tones, and the rounded lips were supposed to give these qualities. Trumpet lips became the vogue, with no thought of natural or coördinate law. I remember one teacher twenty years ago who proclaimed that the real resonance of the voice lay in the space between the outer surface of the front teeth and the inner surface of the lips; therefore, the singer was instructed to "pout" the lips as far outwards as possible, so as to enlarge this space.

As a matter of fact, almost every speech sound can be distinctly and purely pronounced with a smile, but only a very few can be pronounced with the pouting lips. One trial is all that is needed to prove this. This false position of the lips probably has had more to do with poor pronunciation and enunciation than any other one fault. If the mouth is allowed to open freely and naturally, the lips are parted in a half-smile, a slight smile, which does not mean a grin or grimace, and the lips are then free to help form words with the slight alterations in their shape which are necessary.

# CHAPTER V

## Sensation—Diagnosis

Sensation is responsible for much of the confusion in teaching, because teachers try to induce correct sensation in the pupil through imagination, imitation, or suggestion, in order to get the correct tone, instead of asking the pupil to "do" something to cause correct action which produces correct tone, and which in turn will cause the correct sensation. That is, sensation is an effect and not a cause of tone. Correct sensation may be a guide after it has once been experienced by correct singing; it cannot be obtained except by correct singing. We may ask a man who has never eaten an olive what an olive tastes like, or what is the real "taste sensation" of eating an olive. He will promptly voice his ignorance, and say, "Let me eat an olive and I will tell you." The sensation then becomes a guide for future eating.

One of the most pernicious and dangerous obsessions in the teaching of singing is the belief that pupils can be taught directly to "feel" the voice in some part of their anatomy! From this have come more ridiculous fads and fancies than from any other illusion.

The attention of the singer and pupil for the past two or three decades has been directed toward the acquirement of "nasal" resonance. To this end all kind of tricks have been invented to induce the pupil to "feel" something instead of to "do" or "sound" something. The correct sensation of the resonance of the head or "masque" can be gained only by correct singing, therefore by correct coördination of *all* of the breath and voice organs, for the simple reason that resonance is the result of sympathetic action, not separate action. As a matter of fact, the endeavour to "feel" some unknown unexperienced sensation is generally productive of tension and interference. It is the old habit of putting the cart before the horse. Sensation may be a guide after it is obtained by correct singing, but it is evident that one cannot get the right sensation unless he makes the right tone.

Shall we teach, then, by sensation, or by sound and action? Common sense must again answer. The mere change of the manner of breathing will often effect such amazing results that the pupil's ear will be stimulated to new hearing by the new sounds formed and emitted, and the sensation of placement will be experienced as a secondary fact, not as a primary fact. So also the production of certain sounds will cause and stimulate the production of certain resonances and will therefore cause certain sensations, which in their turn, as I have said, may be used as proofs or guides.

This would seem to be a direct and complete refutation of the time-worn statement that the singer must be taught by sensation alone because he cannot hear his own voice. This statement is the height of folly and untruth; first, because of the above reasoning which proves that sensation is an effect and not a cause; and second, because we all know that a totally deaf person cannot learn to be a good singer, simply because he does not hear his own voice. The singer must not only hear his own voice, but he must continually learn to hear it better, and be able to judge of what he is doing more and more keenly through practice and public experience. Whether he hears his voice exactly as others hear it is not the question. The fact that he hears it at all gives him a basis for comparison for all of his effects, and therefore becomes the guiding factor in his art.

So, teaching the pupil to *do* something, to create sounds which will aid in establishing correct action, will cause him both to *hear* correctly and to *feel* correctly. But no amount of urging towards some vague, unknown, unexperienced sensation will bring him either the sensation, or the tone or resonance sought after.

Lamperti taught his pupils to form the voice at the back of the mouth, from whence it was reflected forward. That is certainly productive of two sensations. Those teachers who taught registers certainly dealt with two or three placements and therefore sensations. As a matter of fact, how could any singer work intelligently towards these various sensations for the same result, voice? Again, the sounding of correct tone gives so many sensations, complex as the actions which cause it, that at most the sensation is more or less general, although one sensation might be stronger than another, and may also differ according to the individual.

### Diagnosis

No matter how extensive our knowledge may be, we shall all agree that the principal part of our task in teaching is to find out what is the trouble with the pupil's voice. We may know all about natural laws, all about the physiology of the voice organs and the other body organs related to them; we may know exactly how the voice under examination ought to sound; we may hear certain well-defined faults; but the big question is, "What is really the matter with this voice, and *WHY?*"

If we know what is the trouble, we can find the cure! Therefore, *Diagnosis* is, after all, the chief problem of the teacher.

Diagnosis of the condition and faults of the singer under examination would include what can be heard and what can be seen, and for that reason I have given, in Part II, a collection of faults, those that are hearable and those that can be seen. These faults are all related to natural laws (as I have described, or as I shall describe), and their remedies are based upon these laws and the use of certain sounds or phonetics, which sounds and phonetics are calculated to improve or induce obedience to these natural laws.

The old classification of faults of the human voice in singing included three principal qualities of tone, or three physical defects.

The first was the *tono frontale*, the Italian term for *forehead* tone, what we call a "hooty" tone: hollow, lacking in real ring, or resonance, or sonority, a veritable "hoot-owl" tone, or a street-vender's call.

The second was the pinched or guttural tone, all those sounds which emanate from a pinched larynx, high larynx, squeezed throat, like those of the "neck-tie tenor"; in other words, what we call *throaty* sounds.

The third was the over-nasal tone, what we call a *nosey* tone.

Of the three faults mentioned, the worst was the *tono frontale*, the "hoot-owl" tone, and the least objectionable was the over-nasal or nosey tone. This classification and decision concerning faults inspires an interesting observation regarding what was considered a really good tone. As the *tono frontale* was abhorred, it is safe to say that the hollow tone made in the pharynx with palate raised backward, lacking in nasal resonance, point and ring, was avoided and never permitted any real success to the singer who used it. As the pinched, "neck-tie" tone was second in the list of faults, it is safe to say that the interference of the throat and the squeezed larynx was avoided in all cases, and thoroughly disliked.

As the nasal tone was the least objectionable, it is pretty safe to say that the old singers sang with an abundance of nasal or facial resonance, and that this was an integral part of the real musical sound of the voice desired, and that even an excess of it was not entirely condemned. This means that the two chief resonances of the voice, mouth resonance, and facial or nasal resonance, were recognised and sought after, even if they were not specifically named. It is an interesting fact that the term nasal resonance I have never yet found in one of the *old* books upon the art of singing either in this country or in Europe.

If we keep in mind the principles of coördination in the vocal organs, which coördination begins with the inhalation and breath action, we shall find that diagnosis is not such a difficult matter after all. We shall see that certain visible faults, such as the swelling of the lower part of the throat, the rising of the larynx, the undue raising of the palate, the reddening of the face, the frown, the swelling of veins in the neck, the pressing down of the larynx, the tightened lips, the grinning smile, the trumpet lips, etc., are all induced by improper breathing or false pronunciation, or so-called "local" placing of the tone, all disobedient to the natural laws of the voice organs, and showing faulty coördination.

On the other hand, tones which are *heard* to be lacking in any of the chief resonances of the voice (that is, the resonances of the mouth, head, and chest), tones which are heard to be pinched, or throaty, or nasal, or hollow, or sharp, or flat, etc., must bear these faults because of some physically imperfect action, some disobedience to nature's laws, for there is no other reason possible. Therefore we can at least begin with the breath action with which all coördination begins, and from that trace the fault. But we shall find that there is an even more exact method than this, and that all vocal faults are due to some particular cause *physically,* although the concept of tone or the imagination of the singer may also be faulty, and thereby induce the wrong physical action. Then pronunciation may be the primary cause as well as the breath, and from these two causes we obtain our whole system of teaching, through analysis not only of natural laws of tone and pronunciation based upon correct breathing, but also upon what happens when we indulge in mannerisms of pronunciation, breathing, standing, etc. Our diagnosis, then, must be based upon what we can hear, and what we can see, and our knowledge of natural laws of the breathing organs and the voice organs, and, above all, upon our knowledge of phonetics and phonology. From these things we can not only tell the fault but we can find a ready and certain cure, without waste of time and strength, without undue experimentation, without the use of "hit-or-miss" methods. For a certain physical action will cause a certain kind or quality of tone; a certain disobedience to nature's law will always have the same result in every individual in proportion to the natural quality of his or her voice; certain phonetics or sounds, parts of words, or syllables, will always demand certain actions of the vocal organs to make them, and therefore these sounds can be classified into a system, sound for sound, action for action, resonance for resonance, which will enable us to find the fault and therefore apply the cure or remedy.

So far as I can see, this means that standardization of methods of procedure in the studio is possible, that standardization of teaching based upon natural law is also possible, although tone as tone can never be standardized and we should never want to standardize it, because it would mean loss of individual quality, if it were possible, which it is not. We find, then, that obedience to natural law will give us the natural quality of the individual voice, which is the first thing for the teacher to obtain; that no two voices can be alike, that quality in the human voice is *individual,* while color is general and part of expression, interpretation and art. That is to say that two voices could never be exactly alike in quality, any more than two faces could be exactly alike, but that two singers might sing with the same color expressive of the same emotion or conception. A voice may sing with colors of darkness or light, of brilliance or dullness, descriptive of sadness or gloom, of joy or elation, of victory or defeat, but these colors will always be of necessity superimposed upon the real, the natural *quality* of the voice which is singing, which quality must remain the inherent characteristic of the voice. This means, that imitation of another's voice is death to the singer. He may imitate the *method* of singing, but not the *quality.* He may even imitate the color or expression, but never the actual voice. He may and should imitate himself in his best moments, but never the *voice* of another. Why? Because he is imitating the whole effect of the other voice, he is losing his own quality and tone, and therefore he must of necessity disobey nature's laws and force something in his own vocal machine to produce a tone which is not his. The result is ruin, both physically and artistically.

Diagnosis, then, is the art of seeing and hearing what is wrong, based on an understanding of the natural laws of phonology, breathing, actions of the voice organs,—in short, the complete coördination of the singing act; it permits us to form a definite decision as to what sound or what physical act will induce correct coördination and, by obedience to nature's laws, produce correct tone.

The art of diagnosis includes both what we can hear and what we can see; it shows us incorrect physiological action, it divides sound into its component resonances and shows us what resonance is lacking in the voice under examination, and by our knowledge of phonology it shows us exactly and surely what sound to use with the pupil to supply this resonance which is lacking. For, as all perfect musical sound of the human voice is the result of vibration properly reinforced or resonated, its only imperfection can result from improper vibration or reinforcement or resonation. If we hear or see the causes of these imperfections, we can certainly supply the cure, provided we know the laws.

It may be wise to add here that correct singing never brings discomfort to the singer, nor is it the result of much physical effort. Therefore, when we speak of "intensity of breath-effort," we use the term from necessity, and not because we are inferring that the "effort" is a great one.

In reality, the average tone demands activity, but not much *force.*

# CHAPTER VI

## Hygiene : Exercise—Diet—Operations—Eating before Singing —Fads *versus* Common Sense

"A healthy mind in a healthy body" is the watchword of the singer. Of all people in the world he is dependent upon normal, active, continual health of body, and if he is ambitious of making a real career, secure in his own confidence in himself, a healthy mind is of equal importance. I have no desire to usurp the physician's place in what I am about to say, but long experience and much study perhaps give me the right to give some advice which will aid in establishing a common-sense view of this all-important question.

No man or woman can be normally healthy without regular and sensible exercise. This does not mean over-violent exertion, no matter how "scientific," but it does mean exercise, real activity of every part of the body.

The ordinary "setting-up" exercises practised each morning before breakfast are of the greatest value, are easily learned, and occupy not more than ten minutes if done correctly. In these exercises the whole body is limbered up, stretched, the "kinks" taken out, and the blood is put into gentle and general circulation. A warm shower-bath, tempered to cool or cold, should follow the exercises, and a good rub-down with a rough Turkish towel should follow the bath. Twenty-five minutes will be ample for the whole matter, and certainly anyone, no matter how busy, can afford that much time for the body which helps to do his work.

Walking, lightly clad, so as to avoid undue perspiration, is probably the most valuable of all exercises for the singer, or, for that matter, for any one. Up to the age of thirty-five, boxing, tennis, rowing, golf and all outdoor sports are splendid, but should be indulged in with moderation tempered with caution. Care should be taken to cultivate nose-breathing during all exercise, as mouth-breathing dries the throat, and during exercise is liable to cause "clavicular" or "shoulder breathing," the breath of exhaustion.

Every singer should give special attention to the development of the chest and ribs, but I do not believe in special breathing exercises.

Develop the strength of your lungs and chest by exercise and singing, not by exaggerated breathing exercises which may cause dyspnea, or gross fatigue of the breathing organs.

After thirty-five years, let the singer be content with the less violent forms of exercise, and of these golf is the best. Golf keeps one in the open air for at least two and one-half hours at a time, and the form of exercise is excellent.

### Diet

The question of food and drink is individual, but certain rules apply to all. No man or woman can be normally healthy who supplies the body with more food than it needs or can correctly take care of and assimilate.

Overeating has brought many a good singer to grief, and especially when indulged in at night before going to bed. Late suppers are ruinous to the stomach, unless the food taken is very light and easily digested, and of no great quantity.

The latter is so important, that I would say that the *quantity* of food taken at a late supper is, with a few exceptions, of more importance than the *kind* of food.

Fortunately, people in general have learned much about diet during the past ten years, especially as regards eating many different kinds of food at the same time. The old-time ten-course dinner has disappeared, much to the benefit of mankind.

But, on the other hand, all kinds of fads and fancies regarding food values have arisen, most of which are not well-founded. For instance, fruit is considered by many to be the panacea for all ills, yet many people cannot eat and digest fruit in any form and are better off without it, at least at certain times. Again, cereals are eagerly devoured by many to whom they are rank poison, causing fermentation in both stomach and intestines, with a very serious reflex action upon the throat and vocal organs.

I believe we all need a certain amount of meat, the quantity varying with the individual, but certainly no one needs meat more than twice a day, and if much meat is taken at a meal, once a day is a better rule, especially as the years go by.

A singer's diet is largely responsible for his "singing health." The reason is simple. The diaphragm divides the body into two parts; below it is your food factory, and above it is your air factory; but in spite of the seeming division, the two are connected by the "pipe" of the œsophagus, which terminates with the pharynx, or back of the mouth. Thus the condition of the stomach, inflamed or otherwise, must directly affect the "pipe" and thus the throat and pharynx, while the absorption of certain acids, alkalies, etc., into the blood affects the tissues of the whole body, therefore also of the throat, etc. So we must always take cognizance of direct and indirect effects of food upon the body, and the throat in particular.

The singer's disease, like that of any one engaged in nervous and exciting work, is liable to be acidosis, or hyperacidity, because of the undue and exaggerated excitation of the whole nervous system, which in turn seriously affects the nerves of the stomach. We have just seen how the condition of the stomach may affect directly or indirectly the throat itself.

Therefore it is an evident truth that many affections of the throat, nose, etc., may be caused by the stomach and indigestion. I think it is no exaggeration to say that seven-tenths of the so-called local throat troubles are not "local" at all, but are merely sympathetic manifestations of a disordered stomach, from acidosis, hyperacidity, rheumatism, gout, or whatever you want to call it. Perhaps it would be well to use a term which now every one knows—auto-intoxication.

In other words, every singer must in some measure be a law to himself in matters of diet and living, but all must understand that no one can be well or normal without perfect digestion and equally perfect elimination. A fairly careful study of one's self will show up a lot of very valuable information. You will find out easily what you can eat and what you cannot eat, or you will find out what combinations of foods are injurious to you. This does not mean to develop fads, to deny yourself all kinds of things which you like and enjoy, and which may not only do you no harm, but perhaps do you much good. Eating should be a pleasure, but not to the extent of becoming self-indulgence and causing pain afterwards.

Fruit and starch taken together are often productive of sour stomach or hyperacidity, whereas the same person might eat either without the other with perfect safety. Also fruit may be taken alone, say between meals, and be beneficial, when it will not digest if taken with other foods. I find that combinations of many foods at the same time are generally risky. Too much salt will cause precipitation of the crystals in the blood which form gouty deposits in the joints of the fingers, feet, and even in the region of the larynx, etc.; therefore, salt should be used sparingly by those who have a rheumatic or gouty tendency. Many affections of the vocal organs are the result of gout or rheumatism, and a good physician should be consulted before consenting to operations upon the throat and nose, as many acute or chronic conditions will disappear with proper treatment, without any operation at all. I believe that of every ten operations upon the throat and nose, seven are absolutely unnecessary and harmful.

## Operations

It is true that diseased tonsils may cause rheumatism, gout, auto-intoxication, etc., but it is also true that the gout, rheumatism, etc., may cause the tonsils to become diseased. Undoubtedly, there are many cases when the tonsils should be removed, but there are many other cases when their removal is attended with grave danger to the voice. In any case the tonsil should be "dissected out," not snared or pulled out, and great care must be exercised to avoid injury to the pillars of the fauces between which the tonsil lies.

In the case of a singer, the teacher should be consulted before the operation, and every teacher of singing should have a comprehensive knowledge of the throat and its general laws of action and coördinations, so as to be competent to give this advice.

In general, do not consent to or advise operations upon the voice organs, without some experiment in diet and treatment for systemic conditions. You may save yourself much pain and some money, and perhaps your voice, or the voice of your pupil.

If an operation has been performed upon the tonsils, do not let the singer go too long without exercising the voice, not more than three or four weeks at the most; often, exercise is advisable in a few days. Scar tissue will generally form where the tonsils were located, and these scars are very liable to draw the lining of the sides of the throat to their centres, often pulling on one or both of the pillars of the fauces so as to prevent the free action of the fauces and the palate to which they are joined. I have given in the second part of this book exercises for the singer after removal of the tonsils. (See page 103.)

I have found also a very evident and curious reflex action or result upon the vocal cords, what we might call glottic action, after a tonsilar operation. The approximation of the cords is delayed and weakened, and the voice, easily fatigued, loses its old-time vigor and brilliancy and force. This probably comes from change in the shape and size of the resonance cavity of the mouth and pharynx, from some rigidity of the posterior pillars, as well as reaction upon the arytenoids and the cords themselves.

The voice becomes breathy and weak, the coördination of the resonance cavities is lost, and the singer suffers from dry throat or the reverse, too much secretion from the mucous membrane.

Contrary to general opinion, even in the medical profession, it requires great skill to remove the tonsils safely, and only the best surgeon or throat specialist should be allowed to operate. I have had some cases when removal of the tonsils actually improved the voice, but I have had more cases which resulted in the opposite way. But if the tonsil is secreting pus, there is only one thing to do, take it out, for health is even more important than voice.

### Eating before Singing

To return to diet; everyone, as I said above, is a law to himself or herself, but in my own case I do not believe in singing on an empty stomach. The old rule used to be, to sing one hour after a light meal, two hours after a large meal, and it is still a good rule. Before an opera or concert it is well to eat a light dinner of eggs or chops or steak and rice or baked potato and coffee, with no sweets or dessert or fruit, about six o'clock. If your digestion is rapid, you can eat more than one whose digestion is slow. But in any event, do not stuff yourself before a performance. You need the blood for your brain and voice, and much food will carry it to your stomach. The habits and requirements of food and exercise are individual; what may be enough food for you, may be too much or not enough for another, and the exercise which keeps you in good trim, may tire another to death. Also remember that a little knowledge is a dangerous thing, too often productive of fads and "cranky" ideas, and when you are not right physically, consult a good doctor, and get well. I have in my own way studied medicine and anatomy all my life, but I should never dream of putting my knowledge upon any sort of equality with that of the reputable physician whose whole life has been given to his profession.

Therefore, when I am ill, I consult a doctor and do what I am told to do.

There seems to be no necessity to write about drinking, so far as alcohol is concerned, for the law is ordering for us; but I would say in passing that I have no patience with fads, and prohibition is a fad. If you drink at all, do it in moderation, and never sing with the aid of alcoholic stimulants. It is certain vocal death. I advise this, just as I advise not to indulge in a banquet just before singing. Also there seems to be a climatic difference between this country and Europe, which has prevented our being a wine-drinking nation.

### Fads *versus* Common Sense

The singer requires plenty of sleep, but he should sleep in a well-ventilated room in a warm bed. Open the windows and keep out of draughts.

As for clothing, wear clothes enough to keep warm or cool as the season demands, and don't adopt ridiculous fads about either "hardening" yourself or "molly-coddling" yourself. This may be a good place to proclaim that to be a great singer you must first be a great man or woman, and remember that common sense in all things means mighty good sense, and mighty good sense means a big man or a big woman, big in the best way.

I do not believe that the singer requires a special mode of life. Let him live a normal, healthy, moral life, and, as I said, keep away from fads and notions.

Keep away from throat sprays, atomizers, gargles, nasal douches, and all such paraphernalia. There are times when such things may be necessary, but rarely, and then upon a physician's advice. Also, do not get the habit of running to the throat doctor every time you are "out of voice."

You do not often need sprays, etc. If you are not well, and if your throat is in bad condition, or your voice won't work, look out for your stomach and your nerves, and your elimination. In twenty-four hours you will probably be all right. Don't worry, and above all things remember if you really know your business and your music, if you know how to sing, stage-fright will never conquer you. It cannot, because your knowledge will give you confidence. But if your knowledge is weak, so will be your knees. Even if you have a cold, the throat doctor will not help you overmuch, for a cold generally must take its course, unless you cure it immediately. Medicines do not cure many colds. The best cure for colds is to stay in one temperature for a day or two and rest, but do not keep for hours in a perspiration so as to take more cold. And remember that a lot of food is just what the cold is looking for to become a great big cold. Eat lightly, and take a good dose of your favourite cathartic. Also do not think it necessary to lubricate your throat, during a performance, with cough drops, lozenges, peppermints, etc. They harm the voice. If you suffer from dry throat you are nervous, so try a little self-confidence, take some deep breaths with your chest well expanded, breathe through your nose, and keep smiling. It is wonderful what a smile will do for you and your audience. If the stage is draughty, get some one to stop the draught; but if you cannot, keep smiling, and you will probably not take cold, even if you are not a follower of either Coué or Christian Science. There is mental hygiene as well as bodily hygiene.

Confidence is not built upon formulas or fads, religious or otherwise. Overwork will break it down; so, of course, will illness. If you are ill or out of voice, do not sing, no matter what the conditions. It is always fatal in some way, and may injure your voice for all time. Is one audience worth it, especially when you cannot please them as they expect?

Keep your mind healthy in its action, and keep a decent ethical view of life. Vanity, conceit, pomposity, will do you even more harm than lack of poise and self-confidence. Just because you are an artist you are no different from all the rest of mankind. Perhaps lots of others are also artists in their natures who have never had a chance. Your mental attitude has a powerful influence upon your physical health, but you do not have to adopt a lot of foolish notions just because this is so.

In other words, do the best you can, give the other fellow a chance, and don't *fuss!*

One of the latest fads of singers is to run to the osteopath or chiropractor whenever he or she is out of voice or ailing. I have seen many benefits contributed by osteopaths and chiropractors in cases of cold, stiff neck, tensions of muscles, muscular cramp, etc., also even in cases of indigestion and other ailments, but the habit of running to any kind of doctor or physician for every ache or pain or even discomfort is ridiculous and harmful. And I have seen some very great injuries brought about by osteopaths and chiropractors; bruised and swollen glands, stiffened muscles, even ulcers and abscesses and swollen appendices "bursted," with attendant serious developments. Do not go to doctors unless you are really ill, unless you have some definite complaint. And do not "doctor" or "dose" yourself with all kinds of patent medicines or drugs.

I believe the doctor and teacher will soon find out some interesting and vital connections between the conditions of the voice organs and the condition and action of the various organs of the whole alimentary tract. For instance, torpid (inactive) liver, sclerosis of the liver, infected gall-bladder, intestinal ulcers, an ulcered duodenum, hyperacidity of the stomach, auto-intoxication, chronic appendicitis, stoppage of the intestine, constipation, all

leave very definite marks upon the vocal tract and therefore affect the voice.   The mucous membrane of the pharynx and mouth
is a "tell-tale" of no mean value, and will often show clearly the
troubles existing below.   Vocal coördination becomes impossible,
"local" difficulties are in evidence in vocal muscles and organs,
and we can even settle the qualities of sound of the "liver voice,"
"stomach voice," etc., etc.   It is a matter for interesting observation.   Many times I have been able to send to a physician an
"impromptu" diagnosis or a suggestion, based upon what I can
hear, which he verified by what he saw.

# CHAPTER VII

## Pupil and Teacher : Ethics

The relations of teacher to teacher and of pupil and teacher to each other are of the utmost importance. There will be little opposition to the statement that they can be very greatly improved. I speak chiefly of intolerance and irresponsible criticism. These two failings do more harm to the profession of teaching than any other faults I know of, and they are of continual detriment to the pupil.

Intolerance, whether in religion, politics, family life, or school and studio relations, is the glaring and universal fault against which humanity has been struggling for centuries. Over-specialization has not improved matters very much, nor has democracy eradicated this abomination.

Hand in hand with intolerance goes irresponsible criticism, the most cowardly and detestable of all faults in the profession of the teacher, which profession should be the noblest of callings.

How many times do we hear teachers proclaim that "So-and-so" knows nothing about teaching the great art of singing! How often are teachers ridiculed or criticised by other teachers or pupils of other teachers, without reason and without justice. Teachers are called voice-butchers, ruiners of voices, ignorant, stupid, unprincipled, money-grabbers, etc., by other teachers or the pupils of other teachers, sometimes by pupils of their own who have failed to understand the advice given them. Most of this so-called criticism is simply wholesale condemnation, based upon nothing except professional jealousy or lack of understanding, and therefore ignorance. It is said (to use a slang phrase) that "every knock is a boost," but it is a very poor way of "boosting." It is disgusting, unmanly and unwomanly, lacking in decency and sportsmanship, and wholly detestable. No one has a real right to condemn another teacher unless he has heard that teacher give a lesson. Not even is it entirely safe to judge a teacher by his pupils, although we have a right to judge of anything or anybody by the results produced. But we must be very sure in the case of the teacher of singing that we have heard the real product of the teacher in question, a singer whom the teacher claims as an exponent of his or her ideas and ideals.

Many singers of doubtful ability claim to be pupils, exponents of certain teachers, without any right to the claim. They may be pupils, but not far enough advanced to demonstrate the standard of the teacher in any way.

Also, teachers are blamed for the poor singing of pupils, when the real cause of the poor performance may be due to causes which are not known to the critic at all, for instance some incipient illness, nervous strain, worry, etc. Singers are human beings after all, but the world often seems to forget that fact.

Also, pupils in their formative period are criticised as if they were the finished product of certain teachers. This is where other pupils err to a cruel degree. It would be wonderful if we could combine with our teaching of the beautiful art of singing the inculcation of the principles of fair play, courtesy, kindliness, and above all, the principle of minding one's own business.

# CHAPTER VIII

## Repertoire for Study

A comprehensive study of the repertoire for the teacher and pupil is impossible in a few paragraphs, but in a book of this kind this subject should be at least touched upon. I am planning a book for the study of repertoire for the teacher, so that I shall content myself for the present with a few general observations.

Let us lay down one very definite premise: The singer should be just as good a musician as the violinist or pianist. He should have a good general musical education, certainly comprehensive enough to make him capable not only of reading any music practically at sight, but also of understanding how that music is made. He should have a thorough knowledge of the various schools and periods of composition, of the various laws and rules of classical composition, the use of ornaments of all kinds, a complete knowledge of musical terms, a keen feeling for rhythm and time, for nuance and color, in short, all the various items of knowledge which are included in what we call "style." He must know at least all the various developments since the Renaissance in 1601, and also what brought them about. He must, in other words, understand fully the foundations upon which his art is built, both musically and dramatically. He must be a literary and historical student as well as musical student.

For these reasons the beginner in singing should be trained first in the music of the seventeenth and eighteenth centuries, building his ideas of music and style upon those earlier creations which we call classics, the cornerstone of the great building which has been in process of construction ever since.

It is true that much of the music the modern singer is called upon to execute demands less in an interpretative way than the music of the old masters, for everything in the music of the day is set forth in such definite terms, and all ornaments are generally so completely written out, that the singer can perform much if not all of this modern music with little of the knowledge of the real musician.

Especially is this true of modern opera, with its exaggerated dramatic possibilities. But all this means that the singer has an unfortunate chance to "bluff" his way through all kind of difficulties both technical and musical. How much better he will sing the moderns, with a real knowledge of the classics, and how much better in proportion and good taste will his dramatic conception of a rôle be, if it is based upon a real knowledge of the classic music-dramas of Gluck, for instance, and upon the really great classic plays as well, is a matter easily proved by experience.

It will be understood that interpretations demanding great declamatory intensity put the greatest strain upon the vocal organs, and we know that modern music has become more and more declamatory, and that the accompaniment of either orchestra or piano is now heavier and thicker than ever before. It is therefore little short of madness to allow beginners in the art of singing to attempt to sing modern dramatic works. In fact, no works of dramatic intensity should be attempted until the voice is thoroughly trained and developed and inured to hard work by much practice.

The old music with its great demands upon the musical knowledge of the singer, and its lesser physical demands, affords the very best medium for study and development, with the least danger of forcing the voice. The young singer should study the works of Peri, Scarlatti, Pergolesi, Caldara, Marcello, Handel, Bach, Haydn, Mozart, etc., before attempting the works of the more modern declamatory and dramatic writers. Besides, the works of the older composers promote a feeling for the best style of the singer in developing a sense of real proportion in matters of style, such as the use of the tempo rubato, nuance, color, ornamentation, accent, rhythm, both of phrase and measure, that no modern music could possibly accomplish. In studying the works of the old masters the singer will find the real value of the recitative, which is the basis of the aria, and through the study of this form of dramatic expression he will find the style of the aria, for the one led into the other.

In reality, the study of recitative is the basis for an understanding of the modern aria form, for as the old recitative gave the personal dramatic meaning, so the aria gave the dramatic mood. The former is full of particularization, the latter full of generalization. The former deals with particular statement and proclamations, the latter with general expressions of mood value.

These are the very fundamentals of expression and style. And these are the things which we miss in the modern singer. His early training has little to do with the classics, and therefore his style is based upon no lasting foundation of constructive art.

The exaggerated attitude towards the technique of the singer, the so-called "specialization" in vocal "methods," has made the singer so mechanical and stereotyped, that refinements in style and expression have given place to the eternal question of vocal production.

As we have before stated, the technique of the singer is only a means to an end, and will attain perfection only through a parallel musical development on the one hand, and a dramatic development on the other.

So let the singer sing the best of music in his early days, music which will not force his voice or dwarf his comprehension of the real values of music and drama.

# CHAPTER IX

## Fads and Fancies in the Teaching of Singing

These fads and fancies were gathered by the author either directly from his own experience in various studios, or from books, or from others who have seen and heard them taught. No teacher or book is named. The fads and fancies are all facts in the sense that they have all been at some time or are now being taught.

(1) Placing for nasal resonance in a special locality, generally resulting in "nosey" singing.

(2) Continued use of the vowels AW and OH, causing dark, gloomy tones and "humped-up," stiffened tongue.

(3) Trumpet lips, no matter what the vowel, consonant or word, ruinous to correct pronunciation.

(4) The lowered and relaxed soft palate, destructive of "ring," and causing nasal "buzzy," weak tone.

(5) The locally raised palate, generally causing stiffness of the voice organs, "roary" hollow tone, and very frequently tremolo as well.

(6) The raised larynx, causing "chicken" voice, tight, pinched, unyielding, frequently "white" voice.

(7) The locally lowered or pressed down larynx, causing dark, lugubrious tone with a "swallowed," inactive tongue.

(8) Abdominal breathing, which inhibits rib breathing, and of course ruins correct coördination. There is really no such form of breathing, and it is a misnomer.

(9) The fad of making every attack with the aid of consonants, preventive of clear vowel attack and well-formed vowels.

(10) The avoidance of exercises, and the use of arias and songs as the only medium for development.

(11) The fad that a soprano should never develop good healthy lower tones.

(12) The use of descending scales as the principle exercises, so that head voice will be developed. This in time weakens the fundamental of tone and does not develop the lower tones. Common sense would dictate the use of both ascending and descending scales for the attainment of an even scale.

(13) Take a deep breath, close the mouth and sing the word "come" without opening the mouth.

(14) Here is a formula: "The body brain sends a message to the singing brain, and the articulator answers it."

(15) Another: "Take a deep breath; perceive that the larynx rises; sing without letting the larynx fall. This gives the correct 'pinch' of the glottis."

(16) Approximate the vocal cords two or three times, then sing. (Of course, a manifest impossibility.)

(17) Put a feather upon the floor in front of the pupil, then let him stoop over and pick up the feather as he sings the high tones desired.

(18) Cause the cheeks to become hollow from without inwards, pout the lips as far out as possible in trumpet formation. This will add to the resonance of the voice, as the space between the teeth and the lips is the real resonator.

(19) Lie crosswise on your bed. Let the arms hang down on one side and your feet on the other, until the body feels well stretched. Extend the arms in the shape of a cross. Let the mouth open by letting the head fall down instead of lowering the jaw. Sing AH! This will send the voice in the head, take the strain off the throat, widen the chest!

(20) Feel tired, so as to get relaxation.

(21) Do not get ready to sing.

(22) Open the mouth as wide as possible, because the larger the mouth opening the larger the resonance and volume of tone.

(23) Stand erect, press on the ground with the soles of the feet when taking a high tone.

(24) Distend the nostrils as much as possible.

(25) The fad of psychology and the avoidance of all things physical in the voice.

(26) The fad of lying upon the floor with heavy books upon the chest, which books are to be raised by the pupil on inhaling, so as to strengthen the chest.

(27) The practice of standing in a patented machine, so equipped with arms and contact buttons that any false movement of the breathing organs will cause a bell to ring.

(28) The practising of the most closed OO for several years until the voice is "placed up."

(29) The singing of ZIM, ZAM, ZUM, to perfect resonance.

(30) This one is marvelous: Raise the palate as high as possible, push down the larynx as low as possible, force out the upper abdomen, place the voice against the spine.

(31) The fad of raising the chest as high as possible, never lowering it during inhaling or exhaling, until it grows and remains in this position.

(32) The collapsing of the chest, relaxing it more and more day by day, so as to free the throat from tension.

(33) The making of the "foolish face" in order to relax. After this is accomplished, the pupil must place his hands behind his back, bend over, and chase an imaginary dove around the room. This will relax the "whole person,"

(34) The fancy to sing very loudly before singing very softly, because it takes more breath to sing softly.

(35) The fad of blowing upon a visiting card held perpendicularly in front of the lips. This is followed by putting the handkerchief folded in a certain fashion into the mouth, firming the lips around the end of the folded handkerchief, and singing AH. This is supposed to "put the voice in the head."

(36) The fad of the raised upper lip and wrinkled nose, making the singer look like a "jack-rabbit," or as if he were smelling a very bad odor.

(37) The fad of bowing the head, or making the "goose-neck," when singing high tones. This is supposed to "turn the voice over" into the head.

(38) The fad of separate muscle control, including the attempt to move or relax or tense various separate muscles in the throat or voice organs.

(39) The fad of placing the voice in any one spot of the singer's anatomy.

(40) The attempt to flatten or groove the tongue for certain notes or for the entire scale, ruinous to free activity and to coördination.

(41) The fad and fancy of a certain kind of coughing from the bronchial tubes, at the commencement of the lesson, so as to "clear the pipes," remove all mucus, and improve resonance. What this will do is self-evident.

(42) Standing near the piano, a grand, breathing with abdominal breathing, push with the abdomen against the piano while singing. This is supposed to develop breath control, but in reality only makes good piano movers.

(43) The fad of "vomiting" tones into a convenient brass urn, so that the tones will come "from deep down."

(44) The silly fancy of counting one, two, three, four, five, or more, before attacking "AH." Ruinous to attack, as the tone

should be attacked upon suspension of breath, clearly and perfectly, without delay.

(45) The fad of producing high tones with the aid of the aspirate H, which causes either "flatus" in the tone, or gives a distressing, forcing sound.

(46) The fad of curling up the tip of the tongue towards the roof of the mouth so as to focus the tone. Destructive of vowel sound, because the tongue position is incorrect.

(47) The grinning smile in supposed imitation of the old school. This tightens the throat, whitens the voice, and makes "color" impossible.

(48) Resonance is only established by singing Lll, Lll, etc., with no vowel.

(49) Place a stick between the two rows of teeth to insure correct opening of the mouth.

(50) If the tongue is unruly, press it down with the handle of a teaspoon or a patented silver-plated article made for the purpose. (I am the fortunate possessor of several.)

(51) Put two corks in the nostrils in order to cure singing through the nose.

(52) Sing AH while thinking OO. Gradually think less OO until the AH is perfect.

Is it necessary to waste time or thought or printer's ink on such nonsense? I have stated what would be the results of a few of these practices. Most of the others are self-evident.

But it is sad history of any profession which contains such a collection as the above. Certainly we are living in an age possessed of enough knowledge to refute such questionable methods of procedure, and to substitute for them in all minds something really worth while.

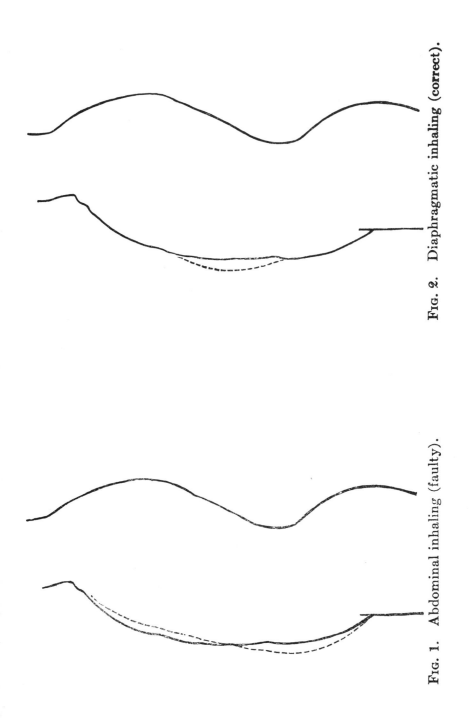

FIG. 2.   Diaphragmatic inhaling (correct).

FIG. 1.   Abdominal inhaling (faulty).

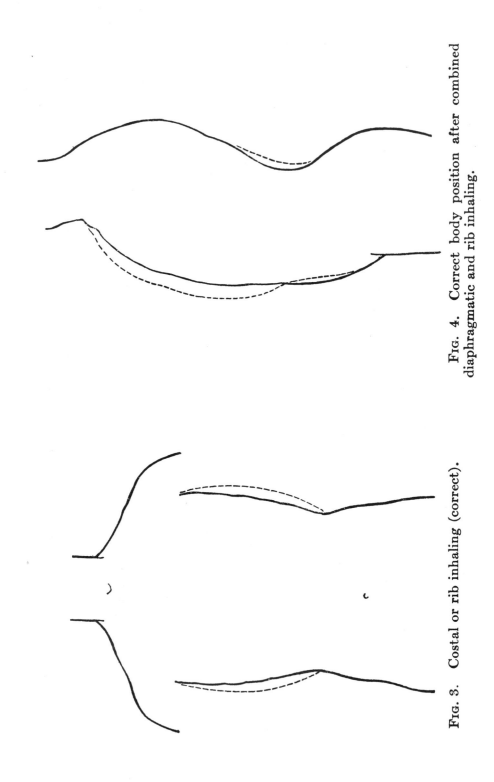

FIG. 4. Correct body position after combined diaphragmatic and rib inhaling.

FIG. 3. Costal or rib inhaling (correct).

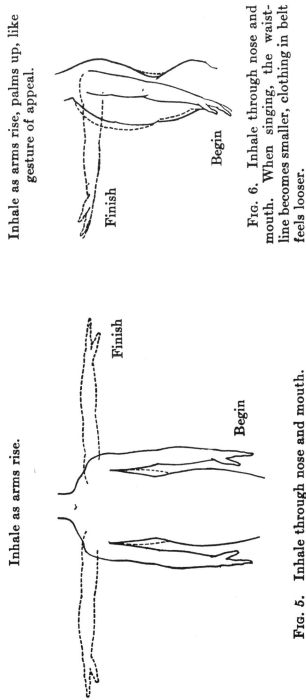

Inhale as arms rise, palms up, like gesture of appeal.

Finish

Begin

Fig. 6. Inhale through nose and mouth. When singing, the waist-line becomes smaller, clothing in belt feels looser.

Inhale as arms rise.

Finish

Begin

Fig. 5. Inhale through nose and mouth.

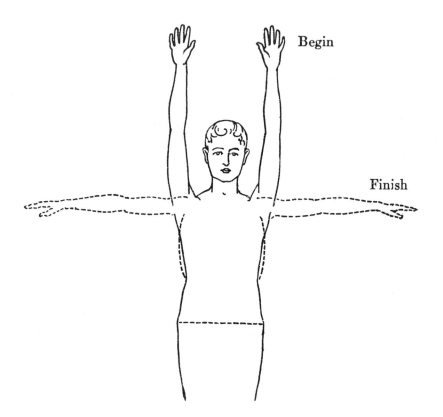

Fig. 7. Commence inhaling through nose; then open lips slightly. Finish with the arm-position marked "finish." Upper abdomen flattens slightly on completion of act of inhaling, on a line drawn through tops of hip bones.

# PART II

## CHAPTER X

### Breath

In the following chapters I have avoided, so far as is possible, technical terms, assuming that the reader possesses the slight knowledge of anatomy and physiology necessary for the understanding of our subject.

There has been more arrant nonsense written about the breathing of the singer than upon anything else except local action and resonance.

The breathing of the singer is purely natural, should never be forced, and does not differ from the breathing used by every normal, healthy human being for any *unusual* physical activity.

There are three kinds of breathing:

(1) Clavicular (the breath of exhaustion).
(2) Diaphragmatic (the breath of life).
(3) Costal or rib (the breath of activity), auxiliary breathing.

Clavicular breathing, accompanied and accomplished by the "heaving" of the upper chest and shoulders, is the breath of exhaustion, and is observable in the untrained person after violent, exhausting physical exertion. It is simply a means of pumping air into the lungs quickly until normal balance of respiration is restored. It is self-evident that the singer never should require this method of respiration, and we therefore immediately and finally abandon it. It should be mentioned, however, in passing, that it is only too often in evidence among singers.

Diaphragmatic breathing is the natural respiration of the human being for life. It is accomplished by a contraction of the diaphragm, the large muscle which divides the body into two parts, which contraction causes the diaphragm to fall, pressing upon the viscera below it in such fashion as to cause an expansion (swelling) of the upper abdomen, outwards and downwards and forwards in inhaling, and the reverse actions in exhaling; that is to say, the upper abdomen flattens as the diaphragm relaxes, and ascends against the bases of the lungs. This is the result of contraction of the upper abdominal muscles, which are naturally antagonistic to the diaphragm.

Let me say here that there is no vacuum caused in the lungs at any time during inhaling or exhaling. That theory was long since exploded. The air fills the lungs as the diaphragm falls. The air is expelled as the diaphragm rises. This is the breath of life. As the diaphragm is attached to the costal or rib muscles, there is a natural sympathetic coördination between the diaphragm and these muscles, leading directly to:

Costal or rib breathing.—This is a natural means of obtaining more air for purposes of unusual activity, and is accomplished by lifting and widening the lower ribs by means of the intercostal muscles, which action is accompanied by a pulling in or flattening of the upper abdomen,[1] expansion of the back under the shoulderblades, a raising and widening of the chest without disturbing the collarbone. The shoulders are never raised, but if anything the points of the shoulders slightly descend.

The respiration of the singer is a combination of diaphragmatic and costal breathing, just as this is the method of breathing for any unusual physical activity, where breath-control is a physical necessity.

Scientifically, we recognize, in diaphragmatic breathing, inhaling as a *willed* action, exhaling as a *passive* action.

Costal or rib breathing gives control over the diapnragm as well as over the ribs, making exhaling a willed or controlled act, necessary for sustained production of sound or voice.

In exhaling during the singing act we find the reason for so much of the existing confusion regarding the actions of the breathing organs. We hear much about pulling in and pushing out, about breath-support and breath tension, about economy of breath, etc., etc., so that it is worth while to try to clear up this needless confusion.

If we recognize that the complete respiration of the singer is concerned with two separate "families" of muscles, the whole matter becomes very simple to understand. Diaphragmatic inhaling causes the upper abdomen, below the ribs, and the soft part of the body between the lower ribs below the breast-bone, to swell outwards and downwards, while costal or rib inhaling causes the opposite action in the upper abdomen below the ribs,

[1] By upper abdomen is meant that part touched by a line drawn from one hipbone to the other. Some may call it the middle part of the abdomen.

leaving the soft part between the ribs under the breast-bone normally "swelled outwards," or perhaps very slightly flattened. This is accomplished without interfering at all with the normal descent of the diaphragm. Costal breathing, however, *does* interfere with the abnormal forcing down of the diaphragm which would inhibit or prevent the action of the ribs outwards and upwards, and which is seen in so-called abdominal breathing. The latter is an abomination for the very reason that it prevents the action of the ribs, which will shortly be seen to be the fundamental muscular action in the whole coördination of the singing act. If we perform the two parts of the dual breathing of the singer very slowly and separately, we shall find that we not only "push out" the upper abdomen, but that we also "pull it in," and when we perform the two acts simultaneously and quickly (as we must when we are singing), we lower the diaphragm, raise and widen the ribs, etc., bringing the body to the position shown in Figures 3 and 4, with the upper abdomen flattened, the ribs and chest raised and widened, the back expanded, the soft place under the breast-bone slightly inflated or very slightly flattened, according to the individual, and depending upon the extent of the rib expansion.

It must be understood very plainly that this action does not interfere with the normal lowering of the diaphragm.

On completing the action of inhaling, or taking breath, we come to the second phenomenon of the breath of the singer, what I would call the suspension of the breath, the pause between inhaling and exhaling, or attack and sustaining of tone. This is one of the most important of all the natural phenomena of singing, and has been too much neglected or ignored. What happens at the moment of this "suspension" is of such vital importance that it could hardly be given too much attention. It is one of the principal items in the whole process of coördination which comprises the singing act.

Before discussing this, however, we must thoroughly understand the act of exhalation.

As we saw above, diaphragmatic exhaling is passive, uncontrolled by the will. Auxiliary inhaling, rib or costal inhaling, is succeeded by controlled or willed exhaling. If this is accomplished without singing, lifting, or other unusual physical activity, the diaphragm relaxes and rises, the ribs fall, and the body returns to an "at rest" position, ready for the next inhalation.

We must remember that there is always the pause or suspension of breath between the two acts of inhaling and exhaling.

In great exertion, such as lifting heavy weights, pushing, pulling, etc., this pause may be reasonably prolonged in proportion to the need of the exertion.

One fact of physiological action is that as the trunk is "firmed" after inhaling, the action of the various limbs and muscles not in the trunk becomes more free, powerful, elastic and delicate. For this reason, when we are going to perform any extraordinary act we take a breath first, whether the act is vocal, such as an exclamation of joy, surprise, a yell of triumph or terror, or is an effort to lift or push or pull, etc. The centre of such act or effort is in the ribs, in the auxiliary breathing act which sets the ribs firmly at the moment of suspension of the breath. It is not directly in the diaphragm at all. The rib muscles are the central controlling muscles of the breath, their action being the centre of the muscular act which causes suspension. It is easily proved. Let the ribs fall at the moment of the "will" to exclaim and you will make no sound. Again, let the ribs fall at the moment of pulling, pushing, or lifting, and you will either be incapable of pulling or pushing or lifting, or you will so far diminish the result of such effort or action as to make it negligible.

This is because of the principle stated above of the co-ordinate law affecting the muscles extraneous to the trunk of the body.

It is this important law which enables us to draw definite conclusions regarding what constitutes breath-control or breath-support for the singer. It is the same as that used by man for any unusual physical action. It also proves to us where co-ordination begins in the singing act, namely, in the act of inhaling; because the act of inhaling, properly executed, causes proper suspension, and proper suspension is followed by proper control and action in the ribs during the singing act, as we shall see, which in reality is proper exhaling, and something more.

Before stating what this "something more" is, let us draw some definite conclusions regarding the breathing of the singer, and then we shall see what this breathing causes, and how it is the vital factor in singing which it is.

(1) Diaphragmatic breathing, the "breath of life," is nose-breathing; that is, we inhale and exhale through the nose, as is generally accepted. Rib, costal, auxiliary breathing is accomplished through the mouth, as when we exclaim or shout; again a self-evident fact, proved by experience. As the singer employs both diaphragmatic and rib breathing, he inhales through both nose and mouth.

(2) Man uses the same kind of breathing for all acts demanding more than the breath of life, namely, combined diaphragmatic and costal breathing.

(3) Breathing should never be forced, for any purpose, and in its action it should be in proportion to the willed or desired action and result. Therefore, there is a definite law governing the breathing for physical action. We could state this law somewhat as follows: The breath act must always be in proportion to the willed vocal act in intensity, extensity, and *time*. By "time" I mean the actual time used for the inhalation and the exhalation. This time may be either short or long, as is self-evident; that is, we may take a quick breath for a suddenly inspired exclamation, or we may take a long breath for a longer and prolonged vocal or physical act, which admits of longer preparation for the act. Perhaps this is the best place to formulate our first law governing the breathing of the singer, which law we shall discuss further at the proper place in this book.

(4) LAW: The *intensity of breath effort* of the singer is always proportionate to the tone in pitch and volume.

(5) As the breathing of the singer is purely natural and the same as the breathing used by man for any unusual physical action, it can be easily and naturally induced; and, as it is part of a coördination, it should not be induced too "locally," but should be spontaneously excited, through practice, to fit the result desired vocally.

(6) Correct breathing will cause the body to assume a certain position, which we will call the singer's body position, shown in Figures 3 and 4. This position may vary in proportion to the breath effort, but never differs in kind, only in degree. It will always give the singer a feeling of balance, never of rigidity or undue tension in any part of the body.

(7) If we inhale through the nose alone, the vocal organs, especially the palate, fauces, etc., must take certain positions in order to admit the passage of air. Again, if we inhale entirely through the mouth, the same organs must assume certain positions for the same purpose, the passage of air. Therefore, if we take breath through both nose and mouth together, the same organs must take certain positions different from either of the above. This means that the correct breathing of the singer gives a certain "vocal position" of the voice organs, which is exactly what happens. That this is of the utmost importance, I think will be admitted. Correct inhaling, then, prepares the vocal organs to do their work, so that we have a right to say

that the coördination of the singing act commences with the taking of breath. I believe that this is not only a matter of relaxation of the voice organs, but that it constitutes a aeal preparation and the beginning of a definite coördination, always in proportion to the willed act, the desired tone or tones. So it might be said that correct breathing prepares the vocal organs to do their work and puts them in a position and condition of "free activity." Let us say here that most of the talk about relaxation is nonsense and has no basis in fact, because we do not perform any physical act through relaxation, but with correct tension and action. This is not to be confused with rigidity, which only retards or makes impossible all normally free activity.

It is true that nose-breathing probably causes more or less complete relaxation of the voice organism; but mouth-breathing or inhaling which accompanies rib-breathing, does no such thing, but causes, for instance, a palatal position different from the relaxed palate of nose-inhaling. This is so true that many teachers tell their pupils to inhale through the mouth quickly if they wish to obtain a raised palate.

It seems reasonable, then, to conclude that one of the missions of correct breathing is to put the vocal organs in a position and condition of free activity, ready and prepared for any willed vocal act. Could anything be of greater importance to the singer?

Again, if we wish to "relax" or "free" the vocal organs, correct inhaling is practically our only means, because, as will be seen later, local, willed relaxation is almost an impossibility, and if often seemingly accomplished, is attended by a causing of undue tensions elsewhere. We shall see that such *local* relaxation can best be effected through sound.

Again, this would mean that if a singer is using the vocal organs incorrectly he can free them and assume a correct vocal position and action only by taking a new breath. Every singer who has studied himself carefully, knows this to be true. Another argument for the importance of the breath act.

To return to the "suspension of the breath," the pause between inhaling and the attack of tone. It is this suspension which finally and definitely causes and fixes the condition of free activity and preparation for the singing act, but which is accompanied by something even more definite and important; I refer to the position of the larynx, the "sound-box" or vibrator of the human voice. As suspension occurs, the larynx, already affected by the act of inhaling, takes its position for singing through the action or "suspension" of the ribs, which, acting through the muscles of the chest and particularly of the sterno-thyroid muscles, fixes the larynx so that the arytenoids and other muscles upon which the action of the vocal cords depends can do their work in tensing and vibrating the cords. This laryngeal position is individual in each and every singer, but must obey the natural law, as given above. This may serve to show how dangerous, not to say ruinous, it is to ask singers to willfully lower or raise the larynx. The position and tension of the larynx and the attendant muscles are dependent, first, upon correct inhaling and suspension of the breath, and upon the willed singing act. It will be acknowledged that this can be induced and perfected only through much practice, and is a first and vital objection to the so-called "local-effort" school. The larynx is not relaxed during the singing act, but works through and with a natural resistance which varies in proportion to the willed tone. It is practically limitless in its variety of adjustments and tensions except as regards pitch, in which there are well-defined limits in each individual; but this is too scientific a subject and outside the scope of this book. It is sufficient to say here that the claims of certain teachers for a certain number of excessive pitches (notes, or even octaves) beyond what experience has taught us to be the natural normal range of the human voice is largely without foundation in fact, although it is true that correct breathing and correct position and action of the vocal organs will materially extend the range of many "short" voices.

We now come to what most singers spend years of their life in trying to obtain, namely, "breath-support," "support of the tone," "breath-control," or whatever you please to call it. It is the real "bugaboo" of the singer. He is helpless without it, he is often self-conscious and nearly helpless with it. What is it, really?

As the auxiliary breathing or rib-breathing furthers coördination in the singing act, as it establishes the act of suspension which in its turn causes vocal position, and insures free activity; as the "centre of effort," as we might call it, is in the ribs, so the attack of the tone is accomplished without letting the ribs fall, as was explained in the matter of the act of exclaiming.

It would seem to be common sense to assume that, as the attack of sound in the voice is accomplished by not letting the ribs fall, so continuance of the vocal sound must depend upon the same causation of position, action and sound. This brings us immediately to what occurs in the body, in the breath organs, during the prolonged or sustained singing act, through a succession of tones or through a musical phrase.

One of the principles advocated by the old school was, to attack the tone without letting the ribs fall. Why? Because of the law given above regarding the exclamatory act. It was found by experience that when the ribs "held," the voice issued clear and free, and that interference with the vocal law was avoided. We now know that this is explained by the laws of coördination as I have so far given them, which insure correct larynx position, resistance, etc.

By the same token, the centre of effort being in the ribs, they must do their work all through the singing act, throughout the sustaining of a tone or tones, that is, a musical phrase.

The question arises as to what actually occurs in the breath organs and muscles during the singing act. It is very simple. As the breath is expelled the diaphragm rises, aided in its ascent by the powerful antagonistic muscles of the upper abdomen[1] which contract and push in and upwards, exactly opposite to what they do in inhaling; the ribs are held more or less firmly not only by their own intercostal muscles, but also aided by the abdominal muscles. This insures control of the ascending diaphragm, therefore of the outgoing air, the direction of effort or action being shown in Figure 4. The ribs hold, the upper abdomen pulls in, and a slight reflex action takes place in the soft spot under the breast-bone which is tensed and pushes outwards, not only at the moment of attack of the tone, but during the sustaining of the vocal act. If this sustaining is prolonged unusually, the *ribs may fall* in order to use the auxiliary breath, but they fall under resistance of the two opposing sets of muscles with which they are equipped. This is of the utmost importance. It simply means that if we prolong the singing act unduly we may be compelled to use the ribs as "expellers" of air, after we have allowed the diaphragm to rise to its highest or nearly highest position.

It will be seen, then, that the chief mission of the ribs is to fix suspension, by aiding the diaphragm, and therefore fix laryngeal position (what we have called vocal position); and that their second mission is to furnish and control a reserve or auxiliary supply of air.

It is sometimes asked how it is possible, if the upper abdomen slightly flattens at the moment of suspension, to flatten it further during the singing act; but this is exactly what happens. As is seen in Figures 3 and 4, the ribs hold, the upper abdomen flattens as the diaphragm ascends, and if we do not require the reserve breath of the ribs, the ribs simply fall quickly and expand again

[1]See note on page 56.

as we take a new breath. This is accomplished naturally and easily with a speed which is remarkable. If we *do* use the auxiliary breath, and the ribs descend under resistance, thereby not losing vocal position, for the new breath they automatically widen as the diaphragm lowers, the body always assuming the position shown in Figure 4. This may easily be seen by making an exclamation of joy or enthusiasm, and then repeating the same kind of exclamation. *The singer should never try to hold out the ribs locally.* Their action and tension are part of a coördination, and they will gradually develop their own natural action. We shall explain the means of inducing this action in the proper place.

I would also strongly advise against "breathing exercises" practised separately from the singing act. Because of the laws already given, because we are dealing with coördinate acts, because of the laws governing the intensity of the breath effort and the relation of the breath action to vocal position, breathing should be practised only with the singing act. It should be borne in mind that any undue or exaggerated attention or effort directed to any part of a bodily muscular coördination generally interferes with that coördination. This is one of the chief dangers in learning to sing.

At the risk of too frequent repetition I would say again that the mission of correct breathing is dual. It not only provides air, but compels and preserves correct vocal position, preparing the voice organs for their work, assuring free activity, and preventing interference.

There is one more interesting observation regarding the breath organs, which is of great importance to the singer, and which helps to explain why he is the victim of certain difficulties. The voice organs possess two series of functions, two families of action; one is the singing and speech act (vocal action), the other is the swallowing act. Correct breathing, as we have seen, stimulates and helps to cause correct vocal action. Swallowing during the act of eating causes the opposite action of the breath organs, that is, a relaxation of the upper abdomen, so that the act of expelling air is prevented or inhibited. This is also simply a coördinate law affecting the voice organs and the breath organs, a very necessary law, a safeguard against choking through the entrance of food into the larynx or windpipe. If we talk during the swallowing act, exciting the coördinate breath act, which, as we have seen, causes vocal position and action, we open the glottis, raise the epiglottis, and food is liable to enter the windpipe and choke us.

Following the laws of coördination further, we can now easily explain why singers who breathe incorrectly are troubled with interference with the vocal act either of speech or song, such as a tongue pulled back and humped up (the swallowing position), a pulled back and unduly raised palate, etc., and a raised larynx.

If we understand clearly the two series of functions of the voice organs through natural coördination for definite purposes, we see equally clearly the importance of the perfection of the action of the breath organs during the sustaining of one tone or of a succession of tones, because of the effect of the breath action upon vocal position and vocal action.

The final phenomenon of this action is to be observed in the finish or stopping of any tone or phrase. This again is exactly in sympathy with an old rule, particularized in what was called the "nota mentale." It is very simple. The pupil was taught to imagine he sang or sustained a tone a tiny bit longer, perhaps the value of a grace-note, than he actually sang or sustained it. That is, in vocal parlance, he "held on to his breath-support" a "nota mentale" or *mental note* longer than the note he actually sang, so that the breath effort or tension ceased *after* the tone ceased. This prevents the "grunt" or gasp which occurs when the tone and breath support cease at the same instant. How often do we hear this in singers, frequently even those who possess great reputations. It is, to all connoisseurs of singing, a distressful sign of lack of control and of undue physical effort. It simply means that we finish a tone with the suspension of breath just as we commence a tone after or practically with the suspension of the breath, and again the ribs are the centre of effort. This completes the action of the breath of the singer, the foundation of the coördination of the breath and voice organs, and enables us to give the following Figure 8, which expresses the whole series of acts clearly and truly.

Fig. 8

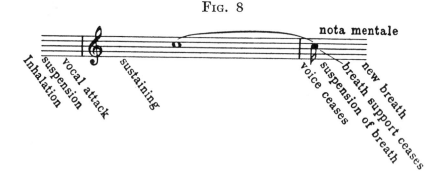

In leaving this subject of breathing I would give the following warnings.

(1) The singer should realize that the breath action should never be forced or made too locally and consciously. It is always proportionate to the desired result.

(2) Breathing exercises separate from the singing act are as a rule injurious, and do not develop the singer's true breathing.

(3) *a*. The coördinate breath action should not be divided. It should be induced by natural and rather indirect means, such as the use of the arms, as follows: standing in an easy, erect position with one foot slightly advanced, raise the arms from the sides, palms down, to a position level with the shoulders, while inhaling easily, deeply and widely, never forcing and never trying to take in a great quantity of air. The lips should be parted slightly. (Figure 5.)

*b*. Standing in the same position, raise the arms forwards, palms up, again shoulder-high, quietly inhaling in the same way. The lips should be parted. This is like the gesture of appeal. (Figure 6.)

*c*. If the singer is troubled with the habit of clavicular breathing, "hunching" the shoulders, etc., let him stand in the same position as above, with the arms raised high above the head without bending the elbows, palms touching. Inhale slowly as the arms descend, turning the palms down as they separate, stopping the descent of the arms when level with the shoulders. If the clavicular breathing habit is very stubborn, commence in the manner above to inhale through the nose, and, as the arms descend, open the lips. This exercise inhibits or prevents the raising of the shoulders and the clavicle. (Figure 7.)

Common sense would dictate that we may practise any of these exercises two or three times without singing, yet always with the *idea* of singing or exclaiming. Indeed, the mere act of exclaiming will often induce correct breathing naturally and quickly.

*d*. Thereafter commence with single tones of short duration, in the easy lower middle of the voice range, not attempting to sustain several tones or a phrase until the breath action is free, easy and correct. It is, on the other hand, unwise to practise exclaiming too much, because it is liable to induce the "catch" breath, or gasping for air.

(4) The breath of the singer or speaker should be taken noiselessly. This can be accomplished only through nose and mouth together.

(5) The mouth should never be opened widely when inhaling; let the lips be slightly parted.

(6) Avoid "localizing" on any part of the breath organs.

(7) Inhale deeply and widely, but easily and without forcing. Do not try to expand the back locally. It will take care of itself.

(8) Make haste slowly, and remember that the art of the singer can be perfected only through patience, time, care, brain, and purely natural means, with the addition of imagination even in the very beginning. Every tone should be the result of a definite impulse of the imagination and the will.

(9) As the singer progresses, induce him to develop the "rhythm" of breathing according to the rhythm of the music he is singing. It must be part and parcel of his expression. This will have an amazing effect upon phrasing.

(10) Every singer should be taught that while he must obey natural law, the *extent* of his obedience is individual, that in this respect each one is a law to himself, that he may exceed another or fall short of another in certain powers, and the breath is no exception. Again, great physical strength may not be as important as it seems, although health and strength are of vital importance to the singer; but how often have we seen delicately, almost weakly formed singers who are able to sustain phrases far beyond the ability of more powerfully built performers. Skill and brains may accomplish far more than brawn and muscle.

It does not require a great quantity of *breath* or *air* to sing a moderate tone, and when we speak of breath effort, we refer to muscular action as well as to the amount of air used.

# CHAPTER XI

## The Vocal Organs and Their Action—Anatomy of the Vocal Organs—Action and Reaction

As the actions of the vocal organs, induced by correct breathing and perfected by correct pronunciation, come naturally as the ensuing part of coördination in the singing act, we will leave the subject of breathing for the present and examine the phenomena incident to the production of tone and speech.

The teacher or singer does not require an exhaustive knowledge of anatomy to understand the laws and actions or functions of the voice organs. On the other hand, he should sufficiently understand what he is dealing with to get a clear idea of what these laws and actions are, how and why they occur, and what the result is both of correct and incorrect action.

Again, he must possess an ear capable of distinguishing all the variations in sound in all of its characteristics—pitch, volume, resonance, quality, and speech forms or pronunciation.

Again, in the following discussion, he should keep in mind that all sounds of song or speech are the results of correct or incorrect coördinate actions of the sound-producing organs. He must remember that all urge towards "local" alteration or correction of action, all "local relaxation," have but one object, the stimulation of more perfect coördination of all of the organs concerned with the production and formation of sound.

He must also be convinced that correct coördination of the vocal organs is dependent, first, upon correct breathing, and second, upon correct pronunciation; and that any undue attention to, or persistence in, or stress laid upon one part or "local" of a coördination, will interfere with that coördination. Before we proceed with our discussion it seems only fair to give some of the principles and empirical suggestions discovered and used by the great teachers of the eighteenth and nineteenth centuries, the founders of the beautiful art of singing.

I would call attention to the following precepts and ideas of the old school.

(1) Let the pupil stand erect in the position of a soldier on dress parade, take a deep breath, and attack the first tone without letting the ribs fall. (Surely instruction in costal breathing combined with diaphragmatic.)

(2) The fauces should always point forward. (Mancini.)

(3) The placing of the head tones of the soprano will be facilitated by letting her sing upon the vowel i (ee) on the fifth line and fourth space. (Tosi.)

(4) He who knows how to breathe and how to pronounce *well*, knows how to sing. (Attributed to Porpora.)

(5) Do not open the mouth too wide, as it ruins quality and diminishes power. (F. Lamperti.)

(6) Let the singer avoid unnecessarily disturbing the jaw during the exercise or phrase which he sings upon any one breath. It ruins evenness of quality and good pronunciation (clear diction). (Lamperti.)

(7) Let the singer avoid practising upon the gutturals AW and OH; they make the voice gloomy and dark. (A general rule.)

(8) Practise neither very loudly nor very softly at first, but an easy *mezzo forte*. (A general rule.)

(9) The mouth should be generally shaped in a slight smile, its natural, easy position. (A general precept.)

(10) Let the pupil "draw" the voice easily and freely at first, gradually developing the *messa di voce* ("swelling and diminishing"). (Mancini.)

(11) Avoid the portamento or slur except as a means of expression, and then employ it rarely. (General precept.)

(12) Inhale from the collarbone downwards. (An old idea.)

(13) Let the pupil imitate his master in his manner of making a tone, but never imitate his master's tone. (Old precept.)

(14) Close the nostrils by pinching them together with the thumb and forefinger while sounding a tone. If the sound is the least bit nasal or nosey in quality the palate is too relaxed and the tone is too much in the nose.

(15) Let the mouth feel full of sound.

(16) The focus of the tone is under the nose back of the front teeth.

(17) Sing as if the breath remained in the body, never as if blowing the breath out. (G. B. Lamperti.)

(18) Attack almost as if continuing to take breath. (Lamperti.)

I would also urge that the object of technique is expression.

## Anatomy of the Vocal Organs

I have purposely begun with the larynx and worked upward instead of following the usual method in vogue in anatomical works of beginning with the upper head-cavities and nose and working downward.

The chief physical organs concerned directly with the producing of sound in the human voice (omitting the breath organs) are:

(1) The *larynx*, situated at the top of the windpipe, of which it is a part. It contains the vocal bands (cords), the arytenoids and other muscles which control these bands, the ventricles of the larynx (Morgagni), etc. The larynx has two parts: (*a*) the thyroid cartilage, the upper part, which remains stationary and which forms externally the top of the "Adam's apple," and (*b*) the cricoid cartilage, which forms the lower part, and which revolves upon an axis passed through its articulation with the thyroid cartilage. As the cords vibrate for higher and higher pitches, the cricoid revolves upon this axis, upwards in front and downwards at its rear, finally in the highest pitches closing the cleft between the two cartilages in front, in the so-called Adam's apple, as can be plainly felt with the finger.

Simultaneously with this action of the cricoid, the arytenoidal muscles pull the cords downwards and backwards, thinning and tensing them in proportion to pitch, and causing a closer and closer approximation of the cords, a closing of the glottis, in proportion to pitch. In the highest tones of the coloratura soprano, and sometimes of the high tenor, the whole larynx may ascend and move a little forward, but this is rare. The natural law is as given above. This extraordinary action of the larynx for the very high voices will be seen to correspond with an extraordinary action of the soft palate downwards and forwards in sympathy with it for the highest tones.

(2) The *epiglottis*, which can fold down closely upon the larynx, and which can also rise upwards and forwards towards the base and back part of the tongue.

(3) The *throat*, including the laryngo-pharynx extending from the larynx upwards to the pharynx (oropharynx), the large space at the back of the mouth, the upper pharynx, or space above the pharynx proper, back of and above the soft palate, called the nasopharynx.

(4) The *tongue*, which, unattached to bone (except the free hyoid bone), works through its muscular rather than tendonous contraction and relaxation, and can move forwards and backwards, upwards and downwards, can widen or narrow itself, and is the chief pronunciation organ for speech forms.

(5) The two pairs of *"pillars of the fauces,"* the anterior or forward pair leading from the back roots of the tongue to which

they are attached, upwards to and terminating in the soft palate; the posterior or back pair leading from the lower sides of the pharynx to which they are attached, terminating also in the soft palate. Between these two pairs of membranous veil-like pillars lie the tonsils.

These fauces or pillars are similar in action; they can widen or narrow the opening between each pair, the forward pair is more widely separated or "spaced" than the posterior pair, the two pairs may be separated by a varying larger or smaller "tonsilar space," or they may be nearly together and almost in alignment when viewed from the front. They are closely coördinated with the tongue, the larynx and

(6) The *soft palate*, the soft veil or fibrous layer constituting the back roof of the mouth, formed of erective tissue or membrane. The soft palate can contract upwards and forwards, upwards and backwards, or it can relax downwards towards the tongue, preventing a view of the pharynx, in most cases even to the point of touching the tongue at its rear. The soft palate terminates at its rear and between the posterior fauces in

(7) The *uvula*, a small, pointed, pendulous formation, possessing the same contractive power as the soft palate. The uvula can contract upwards into the soft palate, practically disappearing into it, it may turn backwards and upwards, curling up out of sight, it may relax downwards towards the tongue. It is closely coördinated in its actions with the soft palate and pillars.

(8) The *hard palate*, forming the front part of the roof of the mouth, made of membrane and bone, immovable and fixed.

(9) The *teeth*, both lower and upper.

(10) The *lips*, capable of an infinite number of adjustments, either in the direction of the smile, or of the trumpet formation. They are largely and radically influenced however in their "shape" by the action of

(11) The *lower jaw*, which may fall downwards and slightly backwards, or which may protrude forwards as it falls, thereby retarding its descent.

(12) The *mouth space* or cavity, affected in size and shape by the tongue, palate, fauces, etc.

(13) The *facial, nasal,* and other *head cavities*, such as the right and left antrums in the face on each side of the nose, the turbinates of the nose, the sphenoid cavity or sinus, the frontal or forehead sinus or cavity, etc.

The forward nasal passages may practically be closed by forcing the breath in inhaling, causing a reaction in their mucous membranes provided by nature to guard against the reception of chilled air; or they may be partially or entirely closed by local or systemic disease.

All of these organs which are not fixed and immovable like the hard palate, teeth, etc., can take an infinite number of positions within well-defined limits; they can move in two or more directions, they can combine in effecting an infinite number of coördinations or combinations relatively to and with each other; but for well-defined purposes and results they are all obedient to certain definite laws of coördination, and direction of action.

As we have already seen, their two chief "families of action" are concerned with (1) the swallowing act, and (2) the speech or tonal act. (We omit for the moment the 3rd—respiration—act.)

From observation, experiment, and examination of the voice organs, we find that these two "families of action" resolve themselves into two well-defined laws of progressive action, which laws may differ in degree according to the desired or willed result, but do not differ in "kind." We also find that they are unfortunately liable to confusion, interfering with the desired result.

We have already seen that both series of actions are influenced by correct or incorrect breathing, and that they in their turn cause certain reflexes or reactions upon the organs of breath.

Briefly, the coördinate swallowing act is as follows:

The tongue "humps" up at its rear part, the soft palate rises backwards against the back wall of the pharynx, closing the nasal passage so that food and drink will not be forced upwards into the nasal passage, or nasopharynx; the fauces widen for the passage of food or drink, the larynx rises, the epiglottis either completely descends over the larynx, or partially descends out of the way of the tongue, while externally we notice a pushing down of the sublingual exterior muscles at the back of the chin; the raised larynx and these muscles forming an almost rigid protuberance in this part of the external upper throat and under the jaw just above the larynx or "Adam's apple." The arytenoids push forward, the cords close and bunch together. It is of the utmost importance to know of these actions, for it is confusion with this series of functions or acts which interferes with correct singing and pronunciation.

During the swallowing act, as we have seen in the article on breath, the expulsion of air as well as the kind of suspension which causes vocal position of the larynx is inhibited, and although there must be suspension of a kind, it is really caused by the falling forward of the upper abdominal wall in the opposite direction to the singing act, preventing either inhaling or exhaling.

The coördinate act for speech or singing is practically opposite to the swallowing act, and obeys a definite law, only differing in degree according to the sound created.

The breath suspension holds, the ribs are firmed, the upper abdomen draws in as its muscles contract, the larynx remains in its normal position in the throat, neither up nor down, the tongue rises upwards and forwards, flattening itself or altering its position according to laws of speech or tone, the epiglottis folds up against the bottom of the tongue, more or less as is necessary, the soft palate rises upwards and *forwards*, the uvula contracts, disappearing gradually with the ascending pitch, the fauces narrow, also in proportion to ascending pitch, and a depression or dimple forms in the front part of the soft palate closing the nasal passage. The lips are parted also in proportion to sound in pitch and volume.

Consonantal sound has its own law affecting the lips, palate, etc.

Vowel sound is sustained or prolonged sound, the consonants are of the shortest duration. We will therefore consider the vowel sounds first. A general law may be expressed for the action of the voice organs for sound. The movable voice organs for the forming and creation of sounds move upwards and forwards in the opposite direction to the swallowing act, except the larynx, which remains in its normal position.

The vocal cords are the vibrators of the human voice. They cause original or fundamental pitch and power. The faster they vibrate, the higher is the pitch; the wider they vibrate, the larger is the volume of sound. But the sound they create without other assistance, as has been definitely proved, is very weak and insignificant. They add to their power, they reinforce their volume (as we say, they gain resonance), by means of the cavities provided by nature for this purpose.

These cavities are the chest, which we will call an indirect resonator, because it is in opposite direction to the sound-waves, which ascend; the throat, the pharynx, the nasopharynx, the mouth, and the cavities of the nose, cheek-bones or antrums, the sphenoid sinus and the frontal sinus, etc., that is, all the cavities of the head above the roof of the mouth. The whole apparatus is somewhat like a two-part trumpet resting upon a sounding-box (this idea emanating from Dr. H. Holbrook Curtis), the chest forming the sound-box, the throat being the pipe of the trumpet, the mouth forming the lower resonator or horn, and the head cavities forming the upper resonator or second horn. The palate and fauces form the principal "key" to this two-part trumpet, regulating the sympathetic actions of the two parts to each other, because of their inherent abilities of contraction and relaxation as described in the list of vocal organs. (I would here caution the reader that the uvula is *not* the palate, although often called so by the layman.)

One of the principal laws of acoustics is, that two sounds of different pitch cannot be resonated in the same resonator with equal result. This means that there is a law of resonation, demanding a certain kind and size of resonator for each sound created. We find that this applies not only to pitch but to quality as well. Again, we find that there is no musical sound of the voice unrelated to speech forms. Every sound we make with the voice organs is part of speech in some language. Then each and every sound or tone we sing possesses pitch, duration, volume, quality, and intensity, as well as speech forms.

One of the actions of sound is that it goes or travels in every direction which is not interfered with. This means that the sounds of the human voice "go" or are resonated in every cavity which they can reach. They are therefore resonated in the cavity of the chest, the base of the air-chamber in which the sounds are made, the throat, the pharynx, the mouth, the head-cavities, etc. We have heard much about nasal resonance in the past years; in fact, this subject has been the chief matter for consideration of singers, teachers and critics. But we can now see from this argument that it is only a *part* of the reinforcement of vocal tone, although a very important part. As a matter of fact, we never see it mentioned in the works of the old school.

Following the argument so far pursued, each tone of the human voice must possess chest, throat, pharynx, mouth and head resonance, no matter how high or how low the tone is in pitch, unless we have some means of shutting off or preventing resonation completely in one or more of the cavities mentioned. That this is manifestly impossible, at least on vowel sounds, we all know, although we may come very near doing so, so near as to cause tones to be imperfect in their resonation. Then each and every tone of the human voice must resonate in all of the resonance cavities provided by nature, and the more perfectly these resonators are used in proportion to each other, because of the law governing the resonation of sound, the more perfect will each sound be.

This deduction means two very vital things. It means, first, that there are not two, three or more registers in the human voice range, but only one, and that each and every tone of the voice is resonated in all the resonance cavities, so that each tone possesses chest, mouth and head resonance; but, because of the law governing resonance, these resonators in their use vary in proportion to each other for each and every tone. We have only to find how this is done. By observation and experiment we find that the lower tones of the voice possess more chest resonance than higher tones, much mouth resonance, and some facial or head resonance. We find that as the pitch ascends the chest resonance decreases, the mouth resonance increases, but the facial and head resonance increases even more. We find also that the vocal organs go through certain proportionate changes according to pitch, and, these changes being proportionate, we find that they are made in accordance with definite law. If we examine this action and its law, we find it to be fairly elaborate, but not more elaborate than other coördinate laws in the human body. We find that as pitch ascends, the cricoid cartilage of the larynx, revolving on its axis according to the changes of ascending pitch, acts in accordance with the demand for pulling the cords backwards and downwards, thinning their edges more and more for faster and faster vibration; that the tongue rises coördinately upwards and forwards, changing the shape of throat and mouth; the fauces point forward and narrow, or approximate; the uvula rises and finally disappears; the soft palate rises forward, never backward; while the epiglottis, rising up against the back of the lower tongue, seems to have a law of its own regarding quality, clear or veiled. More of this organ later.

These physical acts of the voice organs form a coördinate process of readjustment, calculated to so alter the use of the resonators in proportion to each other as to form practically a new resonator for each and every pitch, which is exactly what happens. It seems very wonderful, but nature does other things just as wonderful. The thing to understand then, is, that the coördinate changes of the voice organs for purposes of pitch take place naturally in accordance with the will to make a certain tone, this action (as we have seen) depending for its perfection upon the vocal position originated by correct breathing. It is simply part of a coördination. It is another argument against the "local-effort" school, for no power of the imagination could enable us to move locally and separately any one of the vocal organs into the correct position for the resonation of tone exactly in relation to the other organs.

As each tone possesses all the resonations as described above, then we may recognize chest "quality" or resonance, mouth "quality," head "quality," but *no registers*, for all of the qualities or resonances are sounding all the time, differing in degree or proportion to each other according to the demands of pitch, and also, as we shall see, according to the demands of expression.

This is how tone (pitch and volume) is perfected, reinforced, resonated; but it is created in the vocal cords.

We must now consider quality.

Quality is dependent upon three natural phenomena:

(1) The fact that perfect musical tone is a compound quantity, consisting of a fundamental and overtones (or upper partials, or harmonics, as they are variously called). The more perfect the fundamental, and the overtones which belong to it, the more perfect will be the tone in pitch and quality, the latter being very individual in its characteristic sound.

(2) Speech forms which are made by altering, dampening or "stopping" the resonators.

(3) Other alterations, or "stoppings" of the resonators for purposes of expression which we call "color."

It must be borne in mind continually during this discussion that there is no sound of the human voice in singing unallied to speech forms, therefore we must consider the problems and phenomena of phonology simultaneously with the phenomena of tone, and therefore of quality and color.

Quality is also closely allied not only with vowel and consonant sounds, regarding their own individual color, but also regarding their own individual pitch, both of these phenomena being more or less radical and unchangeable. Because of pitch, which must be perfect, we shall see that vowel sounds and colors for expression are modified in relation to pitch. This is an important factor in pronunciation and expression much neglected and too often only partly understood.

Color, like pitch, is definitely *willed*, and is obedient to law. So are pronunciation, and vowel and consonant formation. If we examine the resonators by means of experiment with sounds, we find some vital and interesting facts.

If we take the normal singer's breath, thereby insuring correct vocal position and free activity, and make a sound spontaneously without purposely making changes in the voice organs, the resulting sound will be the vowel AH, and all of the resonators will be used in accord with the laws for pitch. We shall find that each voice has one tone, generally in the lower easy medium of its range, in which is sounded the most perfect AH vowel, perfect in pitch, resonation and individual quality of voice. We will call this the natural "prime" of that voice. Then all other sounds made by this voice will be modifications of the vowel AH, of this accepted "prime." They will differ from it in quality or color, or pitch, the resonators will be adjusted differently for each and every modification, or as we say "stopped" (dampened, or augmented) in their use; and this is how speech forms are made. As the laws governing the formation for pitch are very radical, so the speech forms are radical, and it is self-evident that one or the other must give way or modify its action. This is exactly what happens, and explains the modification of the vowel sound as the pitch ascends. It also explains why it is difficult to sing or pronounce words upon high tones, the difficulty being exactly in proportion to the radical difference in the position for pitch and the position necessary for the formation of the vowel. Consonants present the same difficulty in an exaggerated form, because the consonants are often even more radical in position than the vowel, and practically are preventive of pitch. This explains why the old precept was, to sound the consonants as quickly as possible, to insure clearness, lack of interference both with pitch and quality. We find also that vowel sounds, which actually are part of the formation of tone, not only demand obedience to their own laws of "stopping" or altering the resonators, which laws they may slightly modify for the desired pitch of the tone, but that each vowel has an inherent pitch of its own. (This has been explained at length in Aikin's book, "Voice.")

Again, we find that the vowel AH possesses normal or prime pitch; that, in relation to AH, AW is lower in pitch, OH is still lower, and OO is the lowest. Again, we find that long Ā is more acute or higher than AH, and that EE is higher than Ā. This gives an interesting division of vowels into two "families," AH Ā EE, and AW OH OO. They represent two opposite developments of pitch, one beginning with a normal prime and proceeding to the higher and more acute, the other beginning with a subnormal prime, and proceeding through the less acute to the lowest. These families of sounds are as closely related in quality as in pitch. They are again the foundation of speech, and possess the fundamental colors which give words their inherent characteristics and expression, upon which again are superimposed the colors or qualities of emotional expression. This simply means that quality (color) is dual, not single, that it has two definite missions, the actual inherent quality of the word, and actual inherent color of the emotion or expression. So the "giving way" or modification of the vowel, caused by pitch, must never be so extensive as to destroy the inherent quality or sound of the vowel. Here we can digress for a moment and find some interesting explanations of simple problems of the singer, long sought after.

If we keep in mind these two "families" of vowel progression in relation to pitch and quality both inherent and "general," we find the reasons for some habits, faults or qualities in singers. The old school forbade the use of AW and OH, which they called the guttural vowels, because they are subnormal in pitch, dark, gloomy in quality, and of course lacking in "ring" and brilliancy. They used OO, as we shall see, for a purpose allied with its own characteristics. They used AH as the chief medium for practice because it is complete tone, both fundamental and resonant tone. They used Ā to brighten the voice, and they frequently used EE, especially in the higher voices of soprano and tenor, to aid the voice in "going into the head." Why? Because of the law governing the resonation of the voice in proportion to pitch; that is, that as pitch ascends, the head resonation increases, owing to the readjustment of the vocal organs as formerly described.

So we can describe "tendencies" of the voice, due to continued practice upon certain sounds, with definite reasons for the results. We can see readily that if a singer practises continually through a prolonged period of weeks or months upon the vowel EE, the voice will get not only too "heady" and thin, but also pinched and tight, because of the very small, radical position necessary to sound EE, because of its inherent pitch, and because of its inherent quality.

Again, if the singer practises upon the vowel OO for the same prolonged period, the voice will become breathy, non-resonant, weak, etc., according to the inherent characteristics of OO. This will be explained more fully further on. So with the other vowels in proportion to their individual characters. Before we do this, however, we must make clear some other very important phenomena.

Just as each vowel has its own pitch and quality, just as there must be and is a definite physical action to cause the vowel, so there must be a law of progressive action in relation to the various acts necessary for the formation of all vowel sounds, and therefore these two "families" of vowels possess a law of action.

We find varied positions of the tongue, fauces, etc., for the various vowels. The tongue moves upwards and forwards for

"AH," flattening itself "out of the way, "so to say, but not unduly or rigidly.

It moves upwards and forwards still more for Ā, and still more for EE. It has intermediate positions for the intermediate vowels such as (M) Ă (N), E (R), E (H), I (T), etc.

This simply coincides with the law for pitch already given, that, other things being equal, the vocal organs move upwards and forwards in proportion to pitch. As the tongue moves forwards it distributes itself sideways; this explains why singers were taught to "sing forward," because the physical action is forward, and causes the sensation of "singing or placing forward."

So with the progression from AW through OH and OO, this action or law is lessened in degree (how much we do not yet know), the tongue narrows and slightly humps at the back. If we examine the vowels again as to their modification in relation to pitch, we find that as pitch ascends the vowels tend to approach each other, to lose something of their separate characteristics, which is exactly what we should expect because of obedience to the radical laws for pitch. So again we can formulate a law.

The vowel sounds modify as the pitch ascends, open vowels modifying towards closed and closed vowels modifying towards open, but they must always retain as much as possible of their "vowel character." That is, they must never become indistinguishable.

It must be understood that the progression for AW-OH-OO does not prevent obedience to the vocal laws already given, but simply modifies the extent of the obedience.

### Action and Reaction

There is no action without reaction. So, just as it requires certain definite actions of the vocal organs to cause or create certain definite sounds, there must be a reaction upon the organs producing or causing these sounds. This reaction results in more or less direct and lasting effect upon each vocal organ, directly in proportion to the action indulged in. The most acute pitches demand the most acute action of the vocal cords, the highest number of vibrations, also the most exaggerated positions of the pronouncing organs and those connected with the alteration of resonation. Then the sounding of the most acute pitches will be accompanied by the most acute reactions upon the vocal cords and in the pronouncing organs. The same is true of the production of color in the pronouncing organs. This explains many cases of fatigue of voice due to the use of exaggerated and false color.

As the vowel sounds differ in pitch, they cause different reactions upon the vocal cords; as they differ in resonance and quality, they cause varied reactions in the resonation and pronouncing organs. This is also true of the consonants, and is more exaggerated according to their form.

Limiting our discussion for the moment to the vowels and the two "families" already mentioned, the reactions upon the cords and larynx are as follows: AH will have normally acute and extensive reaction, Ā more acute, EE still more acute. AW will have less acute reaction than AH, OH still less, and OO least of all. As this concerns the cords, it must also concern the larynx and the muscles which it contains and with which it works upon the cords. Thus the progression from AH through Ā and EE will demand closer and closer approximation of the cords, a more and more closed glottis.

Consequently the volume of the voice dependent upon the swing of the cords, the extent of their vibration, will be less for Ā than for AH, and less for EE than for Ā. Is not this clearly heard? We might say Ā and EE gain in intensity while they lose in volume.

Again, the approximation of the cords for AW is less than for AH, still less for OH, and still less for OO. But AH and AW, being the primes of their respective families of sound, are very similar in volume and cord action.

The OH will have not only less volume than AW, but the cords will have a looser approximation, which, added to its effect upon the resonators, diminishes its actual sound in intensity. In other words, it loses so much intensity that it actually loses volume and carrying power. OO also having the least cord action and therefore the least larynx action, it has the least reaction, and the least volume, as we know by experience.

No one would try to shout upon the vowel OO. We see that actual volume of vocal sound, what we recognize as "big tone," is dependent not only upon the swing of the cords, but upon the resonators as well.

We can now divide our vowels in regard to resonation and action as follows:

AH is the normal, complete resonance and action.
Ā is middle acute or middle high.
EE is the most acute or highest.

AW is slightly subacute or lower.

OH is middle subacute or middle low.

OO is low subacute or lowest. We call OO the non-resonant vowel.

I hope the reader will bear all these simple deductions in mind, because they give the reasons for the system of teaching advocated farther on in this book.

It will already be seen that there is a definite cause and effect for each sound made by the voice organs, always working through laws of coördination. Therefore, if each and every sound has a definite cause and in its turn causes a definite reaction, if we can find the cause we can develop an equally definite system of teaching and singing, and we can also form definite systems for the cure of faulty singing and faulty action, and of many diseased conditions; because, by this means, we can compel more or less action in each of the vocal organs, we can alter coördination or perfect it, we can obtain relaxation or tension, if we only know the sounds which demand the actions which cause the relaxation, tension, etc.

This means that we must teach singing through sound, not through any fads or fancies or tricks, either physiological or psychological. In other words, we can at will modify local action of any organ or organs by making certain selected sounds which directly affect these organs both in action and reaction. This is exactly what we will show how to do. First, however, we must understand a few other facts and principles.

Returning to our two-part trumpet, we find that we are dealing with two chief kinds of resonance, and that these two resonances possess very definite and distinctive qualities. The first, mouth resonance, is the real fundamental resonance of the voice. It depends upon the whole cavity of the mouth in which we "form" the vowels which in their turn form the actual fundamental of the singing tone. The mouth resonance, we might say, is the yell of the voice, the big strident clear metallic ringing sound of the voice. We can diminish it or augment it at will, of course within certain limits. The second part of the trumpet is the head, face and other resonance cavities above the roof of the mouth. Its real mission, besides aiding in pronunciation, is to beautify the big fundamental tone of the mouth. It takes the edge off the yell. It reduces the harshness of bigness and it makes of vocal *noise*, vocal *tone*, by supplying the overtones necessary to a fundamental to make it a musical sound.

Thus these two resonators have definite qualities of their own, and they supply to tone certain quality characteristics as well as pitch and volume—or carrying power. We find that they are in reality a collection of qualities, or colors, made in the various parts of each large resonator. That is, we can say we have two chief qualities of resonance into which we can divide each and every vowel or tone, but that each of these two resonances has its component parts, as pharynx resonance or quality, nasal resonance or quality, etc. As we have already seen, we treat the chest as an indirect resonator, and leave it alone.

I think it will be plainly seen that these two resonators or parts of our trumpet give us two "prime" qualities of sound. The lower or mouth gives us bigness, ring, brilliancy, power, the yell if we want it, exclamations of joy, etc. The upper or head gives us mellowness, warmth, beauty in the sense of tenderness, appeal, sonority, etc.

Within the limits which pitch imposes upon us, these two resonators can work in varied degrees of coördination practically unlimited. We can exaggerate either at the expense of the other, which may promote actual and artistic expression, or may result in mannerism, affectations, etc. We hear the hard, unyielding tone or quality of the man accustomed to command, the strident, coarse voice of the uncultivated person, the "affected," pompous, or over-tender and persuasive tone of the preacher or the charlatan, the beautiful voice of the perfect singer or speaker—each has its own definite *physical* cause.

We can at will divide these resonators in their use, if we know the sounds necessary to accomplish this division, although scientifically we cannot prevent or inhibit either of them completely. But we can do it so nearly completely that it answers our purpose. We can also lessen or augment the various kinds of mouth resonances. Finally, we must recognize the fact that head resonance is sympathetic to that of the mouth, not only directly, as has been shown, but "indirectly" through the roof of the mouth.

So that we have not interfered with or disproved our former conclusion that all tones of the human voice are resounded in all of its resonators, but in varied ratio of degree or amount.

Our final conclusion to which we have been leading by means of all that has gone before is simply this:—To cause correct singing, that is, correct coördination of all the vocal organs, we teach correct breathing to cause correct position and free activity, and then we use those sounds which will cause the vocal organs to behave according to the laws of coördination. Then, radical sounds selected for the purpose will cause local relaxation or tension, will affect position of the voice organs, they will alter, modify cr correct resonation, they will cause the desired reaction upon that part of the vocal apparatus which we aim to affect. That this is the only sure method of procedure, that it is marvelous in its exactness, definiteness and naturalness, I have proved to my own satisfaction during the many years of the development of this investigation.

We are now provided with a system of physical vocal exercise which we will call a *phonetic system*. It enables us to exaggerate or lessen activity in any part of the vocal mechanism; we can practically "massage" any part; we can cure many stubborn cases of vocal fault, degeneracy, and even disease; we can remove many if not all nodes or nodules; we can even improve (if not cure) many conditions without the use of drugs either systemically or locally; and by observation of the results or lack of results of the exercises we can often aid the physician or surgeon in arriving at the much desired diagnosis of the trouble, either local or systemic. We may even avoid operation. I would here make the strongest plea for the coöperation of the physician and the voice teacher. Neither "knows it all." Together they may bring relief to the suffering singer, or they may together arrive at a diagnosis which will show the folly, perhaps even danger, of the further pursuit of a career, at least in singing.

As the consonants are more radical so far as resonation is concerned than the vowel sounds, we find that we "divide" the resonances from each other more definitely with the former, generally aided, however, by the latter. Vowel sounds can be resonated or sounded only with the mouth open. If the mouth is opened too much, this action varying with the individual, the resonance is dissipated and the vowel sound is impure. No part of any sound of the voice, either vowel or consonant, issues through the nose, except the consonants N and M, and the combined sounds NG. Statements to the contrary are numerous and very dangerous and untrue and cannot be proved. So true is this that one of the "tricks" of the old school was to close the nostrils with the thumb and forefinger while sounding a tone. If this closing caused the tone to develop a nasal or nosey quality, the "placement," or production of the sound was wrong.

If we pursue a little farther our division of resonances, we are enabled to make some interesting observations, which must not be confounded with law. As the vocal organs pursue a certain line of action already described for pitch as well as quality, the lowest tones are heard to possess much chest resonance, which may be felt with the hand both in men and women, as well as lower posterior nasal resonance. That is, the tone seems to be very near, almost *in*, the lower back of the nose. As the pitch ascends we hear less chest resonance, more face resonance in the bones of the face, wider and higher up than the lowest tones. Still higher in pitch the chest resonance seems to disappear completely, the resonance of the face becoming higher and more intense, and yet more pointed. We also feel sensations, varied according to the resonances, and often quite complex. The focus of the voice seems always to be *in* the vowel pronounced, in the mouth, fairly well forward, but (as Porpora said) not too far front, not too far back. This is individual; often the voice is not felt forward at all, so far as the mouth is concerned. Again, as the pitch ascends, the sound-waves become shorter, the fauces narrow to take care of them, and the singer feels that the higher tones are narrower, clearer, not so voluminous or so dark, and that they take an upward-outward direction. I know that many teachers will oppose this, but any other procedure results in "pharynx voice," dark, gloomy tones lacking in "the ring" essential to all tones, but especially to high tones.

I would also proclaim here, in the strongest possible terms, that the raising of the soft palate backwards against the back wall of the pharynx, as has been and still is taught so extensively, is one of the most pernicious inventions of teachers and singers. This action is part of the swallowing act of the voice organs, it prevents the proper shaping of the aperture between the fauces, it causes hollow, forced, "pharynx" voice, ruinous to high tones, and is possibly the chief reason for the rareness of good free ringing high notes among modern singers. Even as far back as Mancini we are told exactly how the fauces should be used, and this authority explains very carefully that "modern" singers, that is those of the time about 1784, were beginning to try for more power by means of tightening the fauces and spreading them. The false idea of this action is that the nasal passage is thereby closed, preventing nasal tone, but the slight depression or dimple formed in the soft palate just back of the hard palate serves the same purpose much better, leaving the back part of the soft palate and the uvula free to aid the coördination for pitch, quality and color.

How much we should teach by "sensation" is a much argued point, and one given far too much importance, in my opinion.

At most, sensation is an effect due to a certain action and kind of sound. It is not and cannot be an original cause. Therefore, at most it can be of value only as a proof of action, and after being once experienced, the recalling of the sensation might aid concept in the "urge" towards action.

In all the foregoing discussion of the voice organs and their actions, laws, sensations, etc., we have avoided so far as possible all language which is "scientific" in terminology or construction. The form of statement, explanation, conclusion, has been intentionally made as simple as possible, so that any one, no matter how little versed in physiology and science, may understand. I hope those scientifically inclined will agree that this is an extremely difficult thing to do.

# CHAPTER XII

## Tables of Faults—The Lift of the Breath

Our knowledge of coördinate law, of the various actions both separate and sympathetic of the vocal organs and breath organs, as well as our hearing, enables us to make two tables of faults, "hearable" faults and "visible" faults. Because we know how the voice organs should work, and what their reactions are, we can *see* in almost every respect when they misbehave. So also can we *hear* faults of pitch, quality, pronunciation, resonance, etc., hearing as well as seeing exactly what part of the coördination is most in error. We must also recognize the fact that bad habit "localizes" in one or more parts of a coördination, both mentally and physically, and that this may persist even when some or most of the coördinate actions *seem* to be correct. Faults thus acquired, either through bad teaching or through carelessness and "habit," are often very difficult to remedy, but with the system which we advocate the chief fault can be found at once, the proper phonetic employed to alter the local action more or less radically, which will aid natural coördination, and give the singer the "hearing" of a new sound, or resonance or pitch or pronunciation, etc.; but this should be accomplished with the least possible consciousness or attention on the part of the pupil to a local organ. That is, except in lips and jaw he should not attempt to move or control a certain organ, but should make a sound which alters the position or action of the organ.

## TABLE I

### Hearable Faults

*Tono frontale* (forehead tone, hollow and "hooty").
Nasal tone (nosey quality, reedy, buzzy).
Throaty (guttural, pinched, tight, forced).

> The three principal faults of the old schools.

Flat in pitch.
Sharp in pitch.
Shock on attack, *coup de glotte* (click), *coup de poitrine* (chest).

Gasp or grunt on finishing a tone.

Slurring or scooping attack.

Attack on impure vowel, sliding into correct vowel (very common).

Aspirate attack.

Escaping air or breath.

Varied qualities or colors due to "registers."

Poor pronunciation.

Prolonged or exaggerated consonants.

Closed vowels too "open" (very common);—open vowels too "closed."

Tremolo (three kinds, the rapid "goat bleat," the slow "wave," the middle slow shake, almost a trill).

Dull, thick, dark, gloomy tone.

Lack of ring.

"Breaking" of tone, or cracking.

"White voice," often called "open tone."

"Covered tone" (smothered, congested, forced); a misnomer.

### TABLE II

*Visible Faults*

Mouth opened too widely.

Trumpet lips.

Throat swelling at base above collarbone.

Grinning smile.

Throat enlarging and veins swelling.

Trembling throat.

Pushing down of muscles under chin.

Raised larynx, cramping roots of tongue.

Palate stiffened and raised backwards, fauces widened.

Wrinkled forehead and "strained" expression.

Wrinkled nose.

Humped-up tongue.

Tongue curled up at tip, away from teeth.

Tongue curled down, under the teeth.

Lowered or pushed-down larynx.

Swelling of throat in goiterous form.

Falling chest or ribs on attack.

Protruding abdomen.

Poor position in standing.

Raising or hunching of shoulders.

Too high or rigid chest.

Too much local effort in drawing in abdomen.

Needless disturbance of mouth and jaw (very common).

Non-active lips.

Protruding jaw, forced forward.

Bowing head for high tones.

In addition to the two tables of faults I would say a word about the degeneration due to old age. Sometimes this "old age" attacks singers who ought still to be in their prime. Some people get old while still young in years. The teacher should observe this tendency very carefully when advising students over thirty years of age about adopting the career of the singer. The chief signs of deterioration due to age are:

A slow wave or tremolo due to faulty coördination and feebleness of the breath organs.

Loss or weakness of resonance.

Loss of flexibility, due to lack of elasticity in the vocal organs and a corresponding loss of powers of readjustment of the organs.

Imperfection in pitch.

Shortening in the range of the voice.

A general dullness of tone and loss of vitality.

Sameness of color.

Shortness of breath.

The teacher will find that by practice and experience he will not only *see* the visible faults, but he will also *hear* them, because each visible fault or action is definitely associated with a fault or quality in the tone heard.

Of these faults a few demand special attention here, and after we have organized our phonetics, or "teaching sounds," a cure will be given for each fault.

## TABLE I

The *tono frontale* is the result chiefly of incorrect palatal action, upwards and backwards.

The nasal tone is also chiefly the result of incorrect palatal action in the opposite direction, too relaxed and lowered.

The pinched or tight tone is, of course, the result of incorrect laryngeal action, both interior and exterior.

A voice generally sings flat because the overtones are dampened or are inadequate to the fundamental tone of the mouth. The mouth tone too large for the head tone.

A voice sings sharp because the overtones or head resonances are too strong for the fundamental. Both flatting and sharping are largely due to palatal action, although the larynx is often responsible.

Shock on attack, due to incorrect breath action, poor suspension.

Gasp or grunt on the finish of a tone, due to incorrect breath action.

Slurring, due to breath action delayed.

Slurring from an impure vowel into a fairly pure one; due to incorrect breath action and to slovenly forming of pronunciation.

Aspirate attack, due to faulty breath action and a puff of escaping air.

"Registers," due to faulty coördination both of breath and vocal organs.

Poor pronunciation, due to faulty conception or faulty coördination, which often renders pure pronouncing impossible, no matter how good the concept is.

Tremolo, due generally to faulty breath and vocal coördination, but it is often purposely cultivated, in which case the concept must be changed.

Dark, gloomy tone, due to practice on the guttural vowels AW and OH, to palatal action and breath, or palatal interference.

Breaking of the tone, or cracking, is due to a slip of larynx position after attacking the tone.

White voice or open tone is due to a lack of overtones, as well as to throat and tongue constriction. Palate and fauces are working incorrectly, and preventing correct head and nasal resonance.

Covered tone is accomplished at a definite note—causing a register or change, and gives the effect of compression or congestion.

## Table II

### *Visible Faults*

Of course, faults like a too widely opened mouth, the grinning smile, the trumpet lips (which renders pronunciation impossible), the wrinkled forehead, the wrinkled nose, the falling chest or raised shoulders, the protruding abdomen, a poor position in standing, too high or rigid chest, too much effort in drawing in upper abdomen, needless disturbance of mouth and jaw, non-active lips, bowing the head for high tones, etc., may be done away with frequently by a little attention locally. That is plain common sense. But on the other hand some of these faults are often the results of other incorrect actions, straining, forcing breath action, nervousness due to lack of confidence, etc., etc. For instance, it may be impossible to persuade a pupil to stop wrinkling his forehead into a worried, strained expression, unless he can be taught to change his manner of breathing and of forming a tone.

It may be equally impossible to free the lips from the rigid trumpet formation, unless the attack of tone is changed and a new concept given the singer, both of pronunciation and tone, etc., etc.

The trembling jaw is due to tension in the jaw and throat.

The swelling of the throat in any part is due to faulty breath and faulty attack, causing tensions in the exterior throat muscles, muscles which have little or nothing to do with the singing act.

Trembling throat is due to tension in the throat, caused by imperfect breath action and larynx position.

Pushing down of muscles under the chin is due to incorrect vocal position resulting from poor breathing.

High larynx, cramped tongue, are always due to incorrect vocal position resulting from poor breathing.

Palate stiffened and raised backwards, widened fauces, are due to wrong attack of the tone, poor breathing. It is an unfortunate fact that local control of the palate can be obtained through practice, and many unfortunates are taught these incorrect local actions. The same applies to the wrinkled nose.

The humped-up tongue, the reverse of correct position, is due to incorrect breathing and attack, as was seen in the swallowing act.

The artificially lowered larynx is accomplished with the raising of the palate, again part of the swallowing act, and sometimes is the result of trying to "set the tone deep."

Falling chest or ribs is, of course, due to faulty inhaling and attack.

Protruding abdomen is due to faulty suspension and breathing.

Raising or hunching the shoulders is due to faulty clavicular breathing.

Too high or rigid chest is due to exaggerated or forced breathing and perhaps local tension.

Too much drawing in of the upper abdomen is, of course, very injurious, is very uncomfortable, and is due to too violent rib breathing.

Needless disturbance of the mouth and jaw is, of course, due to faulty ideas of pronunciation, or to mannerisms.

Non-active lips, that bane of American singers, is largely due to careless habits of speech, but it can also come from too much attention to resonance and tone, and not enough to speech forms.

Hollow back is due to wrong breathing, generally to abdominal breathing.

Protruding jaw is due to tension in inhaling, or results from tense throat.

Bowing the head for high tones, very often seen, is of course just a silly idea.

### The Lift of the Breath

Our final phenomenon is what I would call, for want of a better term, the "lift of the breath."

As the pitch ascends, as for instance in the singing of a scale upwards, the breath organs seem to give an extra "lift" or increase of energy at the first note above the speaking range of the voice, seemingly to insure so much breath energy and exaggeration of vocal position as is necessary for the preservation of the co-ordinate action of the voice organs for the higher pitches, the "unusual" or extraordinary sounds of the human voice. This action concerns pitch, quality, vowel sound and resonance. That is, it insures the progression of the actions of the vocal organs forwards and upwards, so that pitch is perfected, the overtones kept in harmonious ratio, the head resonance duly increased, the quality unimpaired, and therefore the vowel properly modified. This is, in the usual vocal parlance, the real beginning of the "head voice" and shows a substantial increase in the head resonance. It is observable in each and every voice at a spot in the scale commensurate with its range, and probably gave rise to the theory of two registers. I have found it to follow a definite law, slightly varying with the individual. This "lift" insures head resonance and makes unnecessary so-called "covering."

In the lyric or coloratura soprano it occurs at C sharp or D.
In the dramatic soprano, at B or C.
In the mezzo soprano, at A or B flat.
In the contralto, at G.
In the lyric tenor, at C sharp or D.
In the dramatic tenor, at C.
In the baritone, at B.
In the *basso cantante*, at A.
In the *basso profundo*, at G.

It shows a very evident increase in head quality at these points in the scale, for each individual voice, yet not anything like a "register."

Of course, as the voice is perfected in its use and resonation, this "lift" becomes less and less perceptible, although it seldom entirely disappears. It is worthy of particular notice, and it is again a proof of one of the theories of the old school. It is principally due to correct breath action, and is not observed in those singers who use incorrect breathing. Its observance will aid greatly in the classification of voices, one of the difficult matters the teacher has to deal with.

# CHAPTER XIII

## Phonetics

The phonetics, or sounds used for the persuasion of certain local actions with the purpose of inducing perfect coördination, are the following:

AH, complete vocal tone, due to perfect coördination, and possessing three sounds in the extent of the vocal range.

AH as in "on" or "hot" in the lower range.
AH as in "Father" in the normal middle range.
AH as in "UN" in the upper range.

Long Ā, used only in the middle and upper ranges, and modifying according to law towards its closed form, EE, but never reaching it.

EE, used generally in the upper middle and higher range, modifying toward the vowel in "IT."

OO without modification (but in singing of course it obeys the law of closed vowels) and sung only "piano."

AW and OH very rarely for only rare cases.

I as in the pronoun so spelled, and used with its natural "vanish" of EE.

M, HM, N, NG, L, T, R, K (N is sung with jaw quiet, to insure tongue action).

Furthermore, the following combinations of the two series of vowels and consonants for definite reasons:

MUMM,MAH, HUNG, NAH, MAH-NAH. MING,MONG,
LAH, AH-Ā-EE. TE-ROO, KAH, RAH.
$\overset{1}{\phantom{x}}\ \overset{3}{\phantom{x}}\ \overset{5}{\phantom{x}}$

Their effects upon the vocal organs in their actions are as follows:

AH, complete vocal sound, is complete in its action in every way; local action is therefore not differentiated. This is the ideal sound for the practice of scales, etc., for the development of perfect tone, from the beginning of study to the end. But it often demands assistance before the perfect coördination upon which it depends can result. It is also normal and complete in its reaction upon the larynx.

Ā long is midway between AH and EE in its formation, immediately demands more local action of tongue and lips, and its reaction upon the larynx is more acute. It has a tendency to raise the larynx unless perfectly formed, raises the tongue forward, and distributes it sideways.

EE demands a still further forward and upward progression of the tongue, a slight closing of the lower jaw, the tip of the tongue touching the lower teeth with increasing pressure. Its reaction upon the larynx is the strongest of all the vowels in intensity, and tends to raise it more than any other sound. It closes the glottis very closely.

The progression AH-Ā-EE induces the natural forward and upward action of the tongue according to rising pitch, while correct suspension and breath action retard the raising of the larynx.

OO, the non-resonant vowel, has the least reaction upon the larynx, and has a tendency to lower that organ, while it demands the slightest larynx action of all the vowels. It can be made "loud" only by modification. As a phonetic it must be used in its pure form.

AW and OH also cause low larynx position, but because of their reaction upon the sublingual muscles, they should be used but rarely, to induce lower larynx and darker tone. They are subject to serious interference in the region of the soft palate, especially upon high notes.

I has much the same action as AH, but because of its vanish and its tendency towards the wider distribution of the tongue, it induces a better concept of the real AH, what we might call the Italian AH. Repeated upon one note or used on several notes it causes action of jaw on the vanish E. Avoid I in "white" voices.

M is sometimes called "AH with the mouth closed." It is not the same, however, but is what we might call the "fifty-fifty" consonant, half boccal and half nasal. It "skips the larynx," so to speak, reacting very slightly upon it, and is made with the voice organs very nearly in the "at rest" position. It avoids larynx effort and tension on attack.

HM is simply the same with the aspirate added to reduce larynx action still further, and therefore reaction.

N is frankly the nasal consonant, with slight larynx action and reaction, and freeing and lowering the soft palate, cutting off much of the mouth resonance.

NG is an exaggeration of N, cutting off more mouth resonance.

L is the boccal or mouth consonant, bringing the tongue into forward and upward motion, closely allied with the action for AH, and therefore forming with AH one of the best syllables for practice for all time, but not for high tones, because it is very "mouthy" in formation, not "heady."

T is used only with the syllables TE-ROO. It aids in persuasion of the vocal action, while the R causes action in the tongue freeing it from rigidity, and the OO loosens and lowers the larynx. It was a favorite of Sbriglia.

K is the palatal consonant, causing a palatal explosion, separating quite violently the palate from the tongue, after they have joined to form it. It causes action of palate, tongue and fauces. It has, however, a strong reaction upon the larynx, a certain shock, and should be used sparingly.

RAH with rolled R causes action in the tongue and often aids in forming the vowel well forward in the mouth.

The combinations are made for definite purposes, as we shall see.

We will now turn to our two tables of faults; and if we know the chief local cause of the fault and know what phonetic causes the opposite local action, either in tension or relaxation, we can cure the fault in the sense that we can alter the sound, causing the singer to both hear and feel the change. This will persuade correct action, and also cause the singer to *hear* the desired resonance, quality or pitch which was lacking in his tone. This in turn will give him a new concept of tone, and he will soon "order" or *will* tones gradually more and more correct both in sound and vocal action. This we might call the law of opposites. It simply means, for instance, that if a pupil sings with a tight, pinched throat, high larynx, "bunched up" tongue, we ask him to sing the phonetics which will tend to release the muscles he is tightening, aiding him also by adequate attention to the breath. If we take the above case we should act as follows:

We should first release the whole vocal tract by correct inhaling several times, until suspension takes place easily and naturally, using the arms as in Figures 5, 6, 7. We might then proceed with the word HUNG, sustaining upon the NG, with mouth open, because this frees the palate which, closely related to the larynx, will tend sympathetically to loosen the larynx and lower it to normal position. The singer will immediately hear the over-resonation of the nose and face, unduly exaggerated, it is true. The H of the HUNG avoids too much larynx gripping for attack; so does the modified UN sound, which also stimulates the upward-forward action of the tongue. We would follow this with its associate phonetic NAH on two or three consecutive notes of the scale, beginning in the lower medium, where larynx tension is apt to be normal, not moving the jaw. We might follow this with the TE-ROO, or with OO alone, *piano,* to further persuade the larynx to give up its rigid tension, using a few notes in the middle of the voice. If the breath action is correct enough, we may now in a few moments allow the pupil to sing LAH on several notes, say in series of three or five, perhaps repeating the fifth. If rigidity persists, we may resort to MUMM on five notes up and down, fairly rapidly, pronouncing clearly, and not trying to sustain the sound of the vowel, letting the M "carry" the sound. This could be followed with MAH or even MY to cause more action in the tongue away from the larynx, inducing the vocal law. Or we could use MING, the M and the NG protecting the EE vowel by surrounding it with sounds which prevent the reaction which EE causes, M and NG diminishing larynx action and reaction.

But in a case like this we would never use AH, complete tone, because of the demands it makes, which are vetoed by the constriction of the singer's throat and his habits; neither would we use KAH, because it causes too much larynx reaction; nor EE alone for the same reason, because it tends to raise and tighten the larynx. We might have to resort to AW and OH, but that is dangerous because of the reasons given.

Again, let us take the reverse of the above case. We have a singer who uses a dark, thick, gloomy pharynx tone, with trumpet lips, palate raised backward, larynx forced down, tongue humped up and pulled back, etc. We might here begin with the vowel I, which will distribute the tongue forward and sideways, bringing the larynx to a more normal position by means of the EE vowel in the vanish of the I, pronouncing the "I" on each note with a definite movement of the jaw for the vanish EE, which will free the jaw and sublinguals, and the EE vanish with the bright AH will alter the use of the palate into the opposite direction. The result will be amazing. Or, we may use MY or MAY or ME, all opposites of the prevailing fault; or MING, if we require more palatal release.

I would here give a most explicit warning. No amount of singing upon the phonetics alone will make any one a great singer. They must lead to the practice of scales and exercises upon the perfect vowels, preferably AH, which insures complete development of the singer's voice in instrumental tone. They are intended only as aids to perfect coördination, and should never be used in teaching unless it is really necessary. Therefore, in the beginner who has never studied before, try to get results by means of correct breathing and natural and easy attack of tone upon the vowel sounds, beginning with the most simple exercises, never demanding too much of the breath, avoiding fatigue, and not attempting anything but the most simple and melodic songs or arias of the classic school. Modern and declamatory music which demands much power or varied color of dramatic expression should be avoided at least for the first two or three years. Let the pupil learn to sing with a gradually increasing and perfecting concept of tone and expression, stimulating his imagination little by little in accordance with his developing powers. Let him practise attack, *sostenuto, messa di voce, staccato,* and the various colors of the voice, the latter much neglected in modern practice. Let him practise scales and exercises in joyful tone, in sad tone, in a tone of victory, a tone of woe; a tone of resentment, a tone of kindness, etc., without words, but with "mood value." These things will all help technique. The phonetics will be found of the greatest value, but of more value for curing old and bad and vicious habits, diseased voices, etc., than for the development of the voices of young untrained singers, who have the advantage of beginning with correct precepts of breath and tone. But even with these untrained ones, we can often save time and insure much more improvement with the phonetics. Pronunciation, forming of the tone with the vowel sounds, should be made a vital part of the teaching of the beginner. *Never forget that tone and vowel sound are one.*

We give in the following tables specific sounds or phonetics for remedying specific faults. The teacher of singing will recognize, however, that some cases will demand a certain amount of experiment, and that often he may have to try several phonetics acting in opposite directions to secure the best results. This is a matter for study and investigation on the part of each teacher, according to the principles and laws already given. Each case must be studied carefully and individually.

Every faulty tone will be found to lack especially one or more of the resonances. Then, understanding the division of resonances by means of phonetics, we would begin by using the phonetic which will augment the missing resonance. After this, use the phonetics which will influence the further free action of the organs which seem to be most at fault, both as you see them and as you hear them. Then follow always with the complete sound as in LAH or AH, watch the result, which will again show you the imperfections still existing, and enable you to continue with whatever sounds you believe will cause more free and perfect

coördinate action.  It is really very simple.  As the voice organs
are very sensitive, they are easily influenced, and will gradually
slip into their natural and freely active coördination.  As this
takes place, the pupil obtains a new concept of tone, and will order
or *will* a tone more and more correct.  As correct tone must come
from correct action, the mere willing of a tone, if the concept is
correct and there is no interference, will produce the correct tone.
This is the way all technique in the human body must be acquired.
It may be the result of imagination, concept and will, but it can
act only if there is no interference.  The phonetics simply do away
with interference and thereby persuade correct coördinate action.

### TABLE I

| *Fault* | *Phonetic* |
|---|---|
| *Tono frontale* (hollow, "hooty") | HUNG, MING, MY, MUMM, AH-Ā-EE, LAH (avoid AW and OH). |
| Nasal tone | LAH, OO, I.I.I., RAH, KAH (slight smile), MY, AH-Ā-EE. |
| Throaty | OO, HM, MUMM, HUNG, LAH, MING. |
| Flat in pitch | Nasal phonetics till palate is free, then bright MY, MING, MAH, NAH, AH-Ā-EE (avoid "big tone" and AW-OH). |
| Sharp | Mouth phonetics, AH, AW, OH, LAH, RAH, KAH, MAH. |
| Shock on attack | HM, MUMM, HUNG, LAH, RAH. |
| Gasp or grunt on finish | Breath suspension after tone ceases. |
| Slur on attack | Staccato exercises, breath action, repeated attack, AH, MING, then EE, MY, MAH, KAH, LAH. |
| Sliding into the correct vowel | (Same as slur.) |
| Aspirate attack, escaping air | Avoid "H"; use KAH, AH-Ā-EE, repeated attacks on one note on AH; also use EE, and MY and MAH. |
| Varied qualities due to "registers" | "Even" the voice by alternate phonetics, both nasal and boccal, and watch breath. |
| Poor pronunciation | Lip action, avoiding trumpet or grin, exaggerate vowel sounds, aid them with phonetics according to interference. |

| | |
|---|---|
| Prolonged consonants | Self-evident, simply avoid the habit. It is easily stopped. |
| Closed vowels too open | Always due to interference. MING, OO, AH-Ā-EE. |
| Open vowels too closed | Due to tensions, generally of tongue, with palatal interference. Use MY, MAY, LAH after freeing these organs with OO, HUNG, TE, ROO. |
| Tremolo (Three kinds) | The rapid "goat-bleat" is due to larynx tension; use TE-ROO, OO, HUNG, NAH, MAH, etc.<br>Slow wave, incident often to old age. Use breath action, bright phonetics, thinner vowel, MY, MING, MEE, etc.<br>Middle slow shake or "trill" tremolo, often due to palate and larynx shaking. Use OO, HUNG, KAH, LAH, MY, until position is attained. |
| Lack of ring | Due of course to palatal interference. Use I, MY, KAH, RAH to get mouth tone. |
| Break of tone, or crack | Larynx is rigid, then slips. Get breath action, use phonetics for head resonance to free larynx, steady it gradually by tones not too loud with OO, MAH, NAH, etc. Watch for lift of breath at proper place—and increase head resonance by means of correct phonetics. Cracking generally occurs on upper notes just over the lift. |

### TABLE II

| | |
|---|---|
| Mouth too open | Self-evident. Change shape to slight smile. Use MING, OO, MAH, NAH, RAH, etc. Avoid jaw action except for M. |
| Trumpet lips | Avoid OO. Use MY, MAY, MING, MEE, TE; avoid AW and OH. |
| Throat swelling at base | Avoid AW, OH. Use OO, HUNG, NAH, MY, MING, LAH, AH-Ā-EE. Use breath carefully; avoid too big tone. |

| | |
|---|---|
| Grinning smile | Self-evident; try to stop the habit, use softer vowels, AW, OH, OO, LAH, HUNG, NAH, change concept from "White Voice." |
| Throat enlarging and swollen veins | Always shows tension of larynx and exterior muscles. Use nasal phonetics and bright vowel MY, etc., after OO; avoid AW, OH, AH, etc. |
| Trembling throat | Sometimes very stubborn. Use alternate phonetics for complete freedom and vocal action, watch breath; OO is valuable. NAH, HUNG, MING, MAH-NAH. |
| Pushing down muscles under chin | Free the larynx with OO, then HUNG; TE-ROO, MING, AH-Ā-EE, LAH. Place finger under chin and try to avoid the tension generally. Breath is very important. Avoid AW, OH and AH at first. |
| Raised larynx | Avoid EE. Protect all vowels with nasal or boccal consonants, as in HUNG, NAH, MAH, MING, LAH. Use also OO in between each two exercises. |
| Palate pulled up and back, fauces widened | Use nasal phonetics like HUNG, NAH, MAH, MING, MY, also OO. Avoid AW, OH, and open AH; HM and MUMM are valuable. |
| Wrinkled forehead | The result of tension and strain both mental and physical. Find the tensions and release them by phonetics. This often comes from trying to "set the tone high" in the head. "Even up" the resonation, paying particular attention to laryngeal position. |
| Wrinkled nose | Also from strain, but sometimes taught to "insure focus." |
| Humped tongue | The most common fault. Generally also draws away from teeth. Use phonetics which cause forward action of the tongue, such as HUNG, LAH, HM, MY, EE, OO, AH-Ā-EE, TE-ROO. Avoid AW, OH. Use also "Silent attack" or whisper, with AH and EE. |

| | |
|---|---|
| Tongue curled up away from lower teeth, sometimes almost closing the mouth aperture | Use silent or whispered attack, OO, RAH, TE-ROO, MY, HM. Avoid L. |
| Lowered larynx | Avoid big tone or "setting of tone deep"; use EE, MY, ME, AH-Ā-EE, MING, LAH, and even a few times HUNG and NAH. Avoid AW, OH. Avoid abdominal breathing. This is a stubborn habit when it has been acquired through bad teaching. |
| Goiterous swelling | Change larynx position and free it at once. Avoid dark voice AW and OH. Use OO, MING, MY after HUNG, NAH, TE-ROO. Inhale quietly a few times through nose with the mouth closed. Also use HM. *Do not sing loudly.* |
| Falling ribs and chest on attack | Breathe correctly and obtain suspension for attack. |
| Protruding abdomen | Change the breathing, also the standing position. |
| Poor standing position | Put one foot slightly forward, avoid leaning back or sway-back, hollow back. Use appeal gesture for inhaling, arms going forward, palms up. |
| Raising or hunching of shoulders | Inhale with arms over the head, as explained in the article on breathing; avoid clavicular breathing, and exaggerate *low* breathing for a time. (Fig. 7.) |
| Too high or rigid chest | Increase action of diaphragm by exercises as above; do not tense the ribs unduly. Avoid local breath action in ribs. |
| Too much drawing in of abdomen | Breathe more easily and avoid localizing in the ribs. Do not pull in abdomen locally. |
| Needless disturbance of the mouth | Pronounce the vocal sounds more *in* the mouth and sing before a mirror, avoiding the "making of faces." |
| Non-active lips | Pronounce more distinctly, using opposite phonetics. Exaggerate the consonants, making them quickly. |

| | |
|---|---|
| Protruding jaw | Often the result of larynx tension, and of incorrect inhaling. Change the breathing, get suspension to free the jaw, and use phonetics which avoid larynx and jaw tension, like HM, HUNG, OO, MUMM, etc., avoiding for part of the lesson the sustaining of sound. Use much activity in all the vocal tract by opposite phonetics, making the jaw very active. You will never relax it by local "willing." |
| Bowing the head for high notes | Simply avoid doing it. It is silly and accomplishes nothing. |

*Return frequently during the lesson or practice to LAH and AH—complete tone—to see what you have accomplished.*

As already explained, these tables are simply direct suggestions which will be found to "work." But of course the teacher who understands the laws and principles concerned, may experiment as much as he desires with the various phonetics, and experience will teach him more and more perfectly how to use them to the best advantage. There is never a local fault which is not connected with or accompanied by other faults. By curing the principal local fault we shall often remedy the others. Remember that we are trying to induce proper coördination of all of the vocal organs, not trying for any one local effort at the expense of others.

Avoid local muscular effort whenever you can do so, but use common sense all the time in everything. Do not tell pupils to relax, because they cannot do so, and even if they do so seemingly, they will not get correct action, which is not relaxation. Do not tell singers to "think" tones somewhere. Avoid all confusing language, and do not play with psychology unless you are very much of a psychologist. Do not tell pupils to open their throats, because they cannot do so without causing all kinds of tensions which will only ruin correct coördinate action. And remember that expression has a vital effect upon technique, and that you should stimulate correct concept and imagination, and therefore imitation from the very beginning: imitation of his own best efforts on the part of the pupil, not imitation of you and your voice, or any other singer's voice. How many voices have I seen go down to ruin by attempting to imitate the great Caruso or Édouard de Reszké, or Lilli Lehmann or Nordica, and others. Great singers have their faults, too, and the Caruso "gulp" or "souffler" of a note has brought many a tenor to grief. This was only a trick of the breath with him, also a means of dramatic expression, and at times was not good or fitting. So the great Édouard could "raise the roof" with his stentorian "open" tones, and many bassos broke their voices emulating him. So others tried to imitate the suave dark round tone of the great Plançon, only to make their own voices lacking in ring and carrying power, until their range was shortened and the voice rendered gloomy and dark. "Oh, wad some power the giftie gıe us to 'hear' oursels as ithers 'hear' us."

# CHAPTER XIV

## Exercises after Removal of Tonsils—To Remove Nodes—Habit and Incorrect Action Due to Disease—Empirical Ideas

Singers who have undergone tonsilar operations or suffered from nodes or nodules on the vocal cords, can be benefited greatly by the proper use of phonetics. After the tonsils have been removed there is always danger of "scar" tissue forming, what is called a cicatrix, in the space where the tonsil lay. There is also danger of injury to the pillars of the fauces, either from actual cutting, or from the "pull" due to the shrinking of the membrane which has been "scarred." The old idea was to let the patient rest for many weeks or even months before recommencing singing. This is readily seen to be a vital error, because scar tissue contracts and pulls towards its centre, and I would certainly advise exercising the voice and therefore the vocal organs as soon as all danger of recurrent bleeding has passed, as soon as the swelling incident to the operation has subsided, so as to stretch the membrane and prevent this shrinking or pulling. This will generally be about a week or ten days after the operation. The exercises should consist especially of palatal and fauces phonetics, those which cause opposite actions, such as "HUNG-AH," "HUNG-Ā," "HUNG-EE," KAH, KĀ, KEE, MAH, MAY, MEE, OO-AH, MING-MONG, NAH-NI, MY. Also inhale through the nose and attack AH or I; also inhale through the mouth and attack AH and I. But avoid AW and OH for a while.

## To Remove Nodes

For the removal of nodules from the cords, the patient should vocalize many times a day for short periods, from five to ten minutes, in severe cases commencing with little more than a whisper. It may be wise to counsel complete vocal rest, talking as little as possible and then only in whispers, for several days or weeks. After the fatigued voice is rested, the following phonetics should be used, very lightly at first and not attempting normal volume or loudness without the consent of the teacher or physician.

Sing HM, with closed lips. After a few trials pick the lower lip with the finger, enough to cause a slight opening of the lips,

while sounding the HM. This will insure a perfect M and all unnecessary glottic or larynx tension will be prevented. Then vocalize with MUMM on repeated single notes, or on three or five
notes of the scale, ascending and descending, fairly rapidly. Be
sure not to "rest" on the vowel, but make the M very clearly.
If there seems to be larynx tension, swelling throat or other danger
signs, use the phonetics to cure the fault as given in Tables 1 and 2.
The principal thing is to avoid any tightness of tone, shock, "open"
tones, and every exercise must be calculated to insure due proportion of head or "over" resonance, with the palate acting
perfectly freely, in no case being allowed to pull upwards and
backwards. Do not sustain any tones until the nodes have largely
or completely disappeared. Most of the phonetics may be used,
always to insure "opposite" actions, *piano*, and in moderate speed.
HUNG may be used a great deal at first, sustaining the sound on
the NG with the mouth open, and following with MUMM, NAH,
MAH, NAH, MING-MONG, etc. Use LAH sparingly at first,
and avoid "AH" and "unprotected" vowels. Also use MAW,
NAW, NO, especially in the beginning.

Do not risk any heavy or dramatic singing until examination
shows that the nodes are gone, and then with great caution. Nodes
can be removed sometimes in a few weeks, but often I have had
to persist with the phonetics for two or three months. It is only
fair to say that some nodes cannot be removed with the exercises,
but an operation is attended with so much risk, no matter what is
said to the contrary, that I often advise avoiding it. It should
also be made clear that many so-called nodes are not nodes at all
but simply formations of mucus. Such "nodes" can often be
"washed off" by the physician. As a matter of fact real nodes,
serious nodes, are rare. They are in reality, as some throat
doctors call them, *corns* on the vocal cords. They come only from
incorrect singing, which causes strain, segmentation of the cords,
and "grinding together." Sometimes incorrect and strained
singing causes the cords to become "fringed," and this is also
dangerous, may result in the formation of nodes, or may make
the voice husky and harsh. Rest is absolutely necessary, followed
by correct use of the phonetics. The phonetics provide what is
practically a system of massage of the cords and their attendant
muscles. They also provide means of loosening the interfering
exterior muscles of the throat.

One of the commonest signs of faulty singing which we now
unfortunately see is the swelling at the base of the throat on
either side or both sides, similar to a goitre. This comes from

forcing the voice with a false laryngeal position, the lower external muscles of the throat and neck being enlarged by continual incorrect use and tension. This kind of forcing may result in a real goitre, and is extremely dangerous. It is very common. Correct vocal position (induced by correct breathing) and correct phonation (induced by means of the phonetics, which will take the effort away from the larynx and the muscles exterior to it) will gradually reduce this swelling, often effecting a complete cure of what seems to be an actual goitre. The circumference of the swollen, enlarged neck may be reduced as much as two inches by careful and intelligent use of the phonetics. This is so important that a word about the exercises beneficial in such cases may be necessary. Use the phonetics HUNG, HM, MUMM, OO, MING, MY, EE, etc., until the larynx is freed from its tension and tendency to "push down." As the palate and larynx are so closely associated in their actions, the freeing of the palate will have a very direct affect upon the larynx in action and position. Dark vowels and tone should be avoided, so keep away from AW and OH. Let the breath action be very carefully perfected, to insure correct vocal position and action, and use the phonetics mentioned until the pressure and tightness and low position of the larynx are prevented. Let the singer develop plenty of facial and head resonance, with the vowel sounds pronounced well forward in the front of the mouth. The swelling of the goitre region will generally go down very perceptibly within a few weeks. If the case is very bad, a physician who understands such affections of the throat should be consulted to see whether the goitre has an inward growth and development. In some cases singing should be stopped for a time. The singer may have a predisposition to thyroid enlargement, but many cases are due only to incorrect singing.

### Habit and Incorrect Action due to Disease

The teacher must exercise great care and patience in all cases which are concerned with acute or chronic systemic or local affections of disease. We have already seen that certain conditions of the liver, gall-bladder, stomach, etc., directly and unmistakably affect the voice organs. Often after the symptoms of the disease or indisposition have disappeared and the disease is seemingly cured, the vocal defects, inhibitions and weaknesses will persist. This is due to "habit," inculcated and fixed in various muscles by interference with their natural functions and coördinations, due to the diseased condition. In other words, false habits caused by disease or illness will often persist after the patient is cured. Again, it is useless and unfair to call a pupil stupid until the teacher knows that the pupil's shortcomings are really due to lack of mentality and not to some definite disease or illness which has in some way caused, by reaction, or sympathetic action, inhibitions of muscle or nerve; positive physical muscular interference which makes the pupil absolutely incapable of performing the actions demanded by the teacher. This is a large and difficult subject, requiring mention, at least, but demanding more attention scientifically than can be given here.

Again, teachers must continually keep in mind that any undue prolonging of the use of any phonetic may result in the forming of a new fault, because of the exaggeration of action and resonance which the use of the phonetic causes. Therefore it must never be forgotten that the acquiring of perfect coördination is the aim and end of all our study. To make this clearer, let us take a specific case. Suppose the pupil sings too much in the pharynx, due to the idea of "drinking in" the tone, of "attacking" almost like inhaling, or some habit or acquired fault. The teacher may ask him to vocalize upon HUNG, followed by MY, MING, MEE, and finally EE, using the opposites of the fault. If the pupil continues too long in the use of these phonetics, he will not only lose the habit which he is trying to change or cure, but he may acquire a thin, reedy, pinched tone, faulty in the opposite direction, and resulting from the vowel EE, which intensifies larynx action, raises the larynx, and causes the strongest reaction upon the larynx. We must use the phonetics simply to release tensions, change directions of action, alter resonances, until we can with safety use the complete singing sound of AH. It is really a very simple method of procedure, based upon actual principle and common sense, and the law of opposites.

### Empirical Ideas

There remains little to be said. But we should not close our discussion without touching upon the dangerous subject of empiricism.

The scientific part of our work is of value only in establishing a more or less definite and complete means of securing correct action *physically*, and, through the simple *persuasion* herein advocated and explained, to help the singer to form right concepts and ideals of singing. As the whole method of procedure si calculated to produce correct coördinate action, natural action and obedience to natural laws, it should lead to perfectly natural, spontaneous singing, with technique never in evidence, but so far obedient to will that the singer's performance becomes a delight in its powers of expression of all that he has to sing. This is the real artist. Expression, then, is the real object of the artist. That this is also partly scientific and subject to law, that it has to do with well-defined limits of the various schools of composition, that it is somewhat standardized, that it must be obedient to form, proportion, good taste, what we call "style," I hope to show in a somewhat original fashion in my next book on "Interpretation."

A few things occur to us regarding empirical methods. Much scientific knowledge, fundamentals, primes, beginnings, have come to us through empirical methods. Singing is no exception. Some empirical ideas are good and lead to correct action, coördination and correct concept. They also stimulate the imagination. The following list, collected during the past years, some original, some from other teachers, old and modern, may be worth giving here.

Correct breathing gives the feeling of elation.

Correct singing is always "comfortable."

When correct action does not ensue, try simply "pronouncing" the words instead of "singing" them.

Imitate your best efforts, imagining a still better and better quality based upon what you have already accomplished.

Inhale from the collarbone downwards. It will aid in acquiring "noiseless" breathing.

Sing as near the nose as possible without allowing the tone to become "nosey."

Close the nostrils with the thumb and forefinger, sing directly into the nose, then tip the voice into the mouth more and more, increasing the "mouth" tone until the nasal quality has disappeared. The result will be a balanced tone, resonant and clear, a perfect "AH." Purely a "trick."

The reëstablishing of sensation. Working from effect to cause through the concept in the brain. Partly (at least) scientific.

The "focus" of the voice is felt in the peak of the hard palate just under the nose. An idea, due to sensation. It may move a little backwards or forwards.

The mouth should feel full of sound.

Attack the tone as if the breath remains in the body.

Attack almost as if continuing to take breath.

After attack do not disturb the mouth position during the exercise which you sing on that breath.

Do not open the mouth too wide.

Exhale through nose with mouth open if palate is tense and high.

Inhale through the mouth if palate is down and more action in palate is desired.

Touch the lower lip with forefinger, pressing it slightly against the lower teeth. It will cause the voice to resound more in the face.

Let jaw fall and rest on the back of the hand to free jaw and keep it quiet.

Touch larynx, to see that it does not ascend or descend.

In all these empirical ideas avoid local action as much as possible. Most of these ideas come from various teachers of years gone by.

The effect of the correct act of inhaling upon the vocal tract is of the utmost importance, but it also may be accompanied by the danger of making the singer too conscious of his breathing. But this is a danger which attends any physical act. When tensions are obstinate and the phonetics do not give as direct and immediate results as are desired, try to induce general, free, co-ordinate vocal action by means of the breath act of preparation. It is surprising what this will accomplish.

Again, I would give a warning. The phonetics, due to the extreme sensitiveness of the voice organs, act as "releases" or "inducers" of action. They should be followed by easy short exercises and scales sung on the pure vowels, preferably AH.

Above everything, do not indulge in all kinds of tricks in teaching just because you hope for instantaneous results. I hope the collection of "fads and fancies" given in the first half of this book will help to show the folly, not to say dishonesty, of using such nonsense.

# CHAPTER XV

## Ethics

It is the most serious duty of the teacher of singing to advise pupils honestly about their futures. It is true that people have a right to study whether a teacher thinks they are sufficiently talented to succeed as professional singers or not. But the teacher's opinion should be expressed in definite terms, so that the status of the pupil is made very clear to both teacher and pupil, and to parents or guardians.

No pupil should be allowed to continue spending money upon a voice and musical talent insufficient for a career, if thereby the teacher is fostering a hope of that career in the mind and ambition of the pupil. But it is a self-evident fact that many people may desire to study the art of singing without any intention of pursuing the career of a public or professional singer, simply for their own enjoyment or education, and they become very valuable aids to the musical life of their community by doing so.

I should also fail in my duty to the musical profession if I did not include here a plea for higher ethical standards among both teachers and pupils. The newly formed American Academy of Teachers of Singing has proved that it is both possible and beneficial for teachers to meet at regular and appointed times to discuss matters pertaining to their profession. These men have learned much from each other both professionally and ethically, and they have formed new and lasting friendships with each other. Rivalry and competition are healthy aids to any profession, if the rivals are gentlemen and "good sportsmen," are ladies and "good sportswomen."

But irresponsible, hateful and envious criticism is unfair, undignified and wholly detestable. Have we not had too much of it in our profession?

The pupil also is often to blame for this same kind of unfounded criticism, both of other teachers than his own, and of other pupils who like himself are struggling for success. And too often the pupil is ready to blame his teacher for all his own shortcomings. Discipline in the studio is essential, and the cordial understanding between teacher and pupil should never be allowed to weaken the respect of the latter for the former.

A new danger has arisen recently which is to be deplored. Pupils are looking to the teacher more and more for opportunities for public appearance or for employment. The teacher of singing is not a manager, but a teacher. He cannot fill both positions without loss to one or the other. As competition in the profession grows more keen this danger will increase, unless the teachers take some definite stand. Pupils should be made to appreciate the fact, a true fact, that if they are really competent to excel, opportunity will come. We hear an oft-repeated complaint that the American singer has no chance in his own country, but I think it is much exaggerated. The career of the singer is a hard one, hard in preparation, difficult in its continuance, but so is every other career. And certainly the career of the singer offers as large a monetary reward as does that of the doctor, lawyer, clergyman, etc.

It is to be regretted that the education of the modern singer is suffering from two unfortunate results of modern conditions, (1) lack of thoroughness due to haste and lack of time, and (2) the high cost of lessons and living, which is the direct cause of the hurry. So it is all the more essential to save all the time possible in the process of training and developing the voice. At the same time we must remember that a certain length of time, varying with the individual, is absolutely necessary, and no matter what existing conditions are, we still have to face the unyielding fact that real ability can come only through hard, patient, prolonged endeavour. I would say that few pupils can become real singers, let alone great singers, with less than five years of close application and unselfish devotion to their art.

It would have been much easier to write this book if I could have made it twice as long and employed scientific language to make my meaning certain. To condense any knowledge is a difficult procedure; to express scientific reasoning and facts in everyday language is a hard task. But it is better to go straight to a point, and I detest verbosity. Brevity is the soul of wit, real facts demand few words, and no wordy explanation is of value, one that makes us feel "you cannot see the forest for the trees."

Again let me say that I do not know it all. There are many riddles in my notebooks for future investigation, most of which I shall never clear up or solve. Life is short. But I want the reader to know that I have written this book with much humility, aware of my own shortcomings, hoping only that it may help our profession in some humble but valuable way.

I have tried not to "harp" on old tiresome questions, I have also tried to state the various laws as clearly and tritely as possible. Perhaps I have omitted many things which others would like to discuss. But I have followed out a plan definitely made and arranged to express what I believe is a sane, sure way of dealing with the technical problems of the singer.

May I add once more that no teaching of an art can be entirely mechanical, nor can it be entirely scientific. It must return again and again to the art itself for further inspiration, in order that Technique, rightly developed, may become the servant of Expression and Interpretation.

---

The following code of ethics adopted by The American Academy of Teachers of Singing is given with the hope that all teachers will observe it in the practice of their profession.

## PREAMBLE

We, members of The American Academy of Teachers of Singing, citizens of the United States, dedicate this code of ethics to the advancement of vocal art.

## CODE

ARTICLE 1. Members of the Academy, in accordance with Article 2 of the Constitution, agree to further: (1) the establishment of a code which will improve the ethical principles and practice of the profession; (2) the spreading of knowledge and culture, and (3) the promotion of coöperation and good fellowship.

ARTICLE 2. Members of the Academy assume the obligation to promote the teaching of singing, not primarily as a commercial project, but as a means of culture; to maintain and increase the prestige of the art of singing; and to conform to the standards of correct professional conduct as instructors, advisers, and gentlemen.

ARTICLE 3. The teacher of singing should possess both character and education.

ARTICLE 4. Any unprofessional, dishonest, or corrupt conduct on the part of teacher or pupil should be reported to the Academy.

ARTICLE 5. Any pupil who has deliberately failed to pay his just indebtedness shall be reported to the Academy, and shall not be accepted as a pupil by any other member until his debt is paid.

ARTICLE 6. Any specific promise by the teacher that leads the student to false hopes of a career is a breach of ethics and integrity.

ARTICLE 7. A minimum of one year of continuous instruction shall warrant the teacher in claiming the student as a pupil. But fairness must be practiced in the proper recognition of helpful services rendered by former teachers, and derogatory statements avoided. Furthermore, dignity and a scrupulous adherence to facts in advertising shall always be observed.

ARTICLE 8. Teachers should treat their pupils with consideration and patience, inculcating in them respect for their art.

ARTICLE 9. In voice trials the duty of the teacher is to diagnose the case impartially. Therefore it is suggested that at the outset the student be requested not to disclose the name of any former teacher. In all instances an honest opinion should be given the student.

ARTICLF 10. Punctuality is incumbent upon teacher and pupil. Pupils should be held responsible for the time originally reserved, except in rare emergency.

# CHAPTER XVI

## Exercises

The exercises given at the end of this book are all that are necessary for the early training of the voice, as well as for the cure of those singers who have acquired faulty habits of singing. Vocalises such as those in use in most studios, melodies without words by Concone, Lamperti, Panofka, Marchesi and others are all valuable, but their use should not be unduly prolonged. Rather allow the pupil to sing easy songs and arias, good music, never "trash" or "popular" songs. When the pupil is beginning to be able to sing somewhat correctly, stimulate his artistic sense, his imagination and interpretation, as well as his acquirement of correct pronunciation, by the singing of such pieces. Let American pupils practise in their own language as well as in Italian. Later they may attempt the German and French tongues, which are essential for their career. Perhaps in the future we shall use chiefly our own English speech in singing. I hope so. At present our audiences in both concert and opera listen in sublime ignorance to almost every language but their own. Yet we have improved in this regard, so there is hope for the future. At any rate, I have no desire to enter upon this much trampled battlefield.

The exercises are all given in the key of C, and may be transposed higher or lower as the range of the voice demands. Common sense dictates the development of the middle range of each voice in the beginning of study. Almost every voice has one or two tones (notes) more free, resonant and correctly produced than others. Practice may be begun with these notes. Ascending and descending exercises are of equal importance. Single notes and short exercises should be used at first, so as not to demand too much of the breath organs. Quality is of more importance than quantity, and the ability to sing *piano* must go hand in hand with power. The teacher must both see and hear what the pupil is doing all the time. Descending scales should in general be commenced at a note just above the "lift of the breath"; for instance, in the soprano, at D or E, fourth line and fourth space. Other voices according to the table given on page 90.

Rapid arpeggios are not to be used until the pupil has a definite idea of what he is trying to do, because he will not produce half of the notes correctly, and such rapid exercises will only result in carelessness and slovenliness of execution. Ascending scales naturally possess the danger of "carrying up" too much of the lower quality and weight of the voice, while descending scales run the opposite danger of carrying down the head quality too low, thereby weakening the fundamental of the tone.

Swelling and diminishing the tone should be practised as soon as the pupil has a fair control of the breath. This exercise is of the utmost importance. Generally speaking, "falsetto," the artificial or womanish voice of the man, should be avoided, although at times it may be valuable to give the idea of "head" quality. *Sotto voce*, on the other hand, should be acquired as soon as the singer can use the breath well. As already shown, this is the tone made by almost abandoning the breath-support, as its name signifies. The singer should be taught to bring the whole "breath action" gradually into activity, while holding a note, until the tone may be developed to the full power of the voice and diminished back to the *sotto voce*. This is necessary for both men and women.

Remember that no one exercise or "fad" or phonetic is a panacea for all ills. The phonetics should not be carried higher than a note or two above the lift of the breath, except in rare instances, because of the exaggeration of the vocal law in the higher range. So in the very radical phonetics like HUNG, NG, HM, all consonantal sounds, limit their use to the notes just above the "lift." High notes should be developed upon the vowel sounds, generally on scales, after preparing the vocal organs to act in obedience to the laws of coördination. If the singer gets a good start on the middle notes in this way, the chances are that the obedience to natural law will continue to the higher notes, more and more perfectly through practice. Let the vowel sound modify duly for the higher notes, but not too much.

Exercises 1 to 19 are best adapted for the radical phonetics. The other exercises should be used with vowel sounds. Combinations of phonetics may be used, sounding two or more phonetics on single notes, or on several notes.

In using HUNG, the voice must sustain always upon the NG, with the mouth open, pronouncing or attacking the word only once for each exercise. The other phonetics employing consonants should be used, a syllable for each note.

Let the pupil "bind" notes together without slurring, developing a perfect legato; also insist upon the practice of repeated notes, getting a better, cleaner attack and finish of each note.

Use staccato frequently both for men and women. It causes better and better attack, uniformity of quality, breath control, and ease in singing. It is much neglected. It should not be overdone, especially with men. Do not allow "plunging" for high notes. Rather let the pupil attack the high note *piano*, or go from a low note to the higher notes *piano*, then swell the high note. Do not use *portamento* at first. It may induce objectionable slurring or scooping. As soon as possible develop the full extent of the voice in range and power with the vowel sounds, remembering that AH is complete sound, but do not attempt anything too soon and without caution. A forced voice is a sick voice, and unnecessary rest means loss of time.

Cultivate facility and rapidity of execution by degrees, but make this an important part of study. The various slower exercises given may be sung faster and faster by degrees, until short and long scales can be sung with great rapidity.

Also turns, ornamental figures of all kinds should be practised by all voices, whether coloratura or not. Agility aids in acquiring evenness of quality through the vocal range. It is too much neglected to-day in the search after power. Agility in exercises does for the voice what light agile exercises do for the body. Too much sustained singing will make the voice heavy and dull.

The last thing to put in the voice is power. Power gives the sensation of singing "down on the breath" extremely, also the feeling of singing a little farther back in the mouth, what we call a "full-throated" sound. It is somewhat allied to the feeling of the modified vowel, with the largest and heaviest fundamental of the mouth, and the strongest resonance of the "masque." Of course the danger, even for experienced singers, is the tendency to sing too dark and heavy, until the throat is tense and distended. If power is attempted with white voice, the result is vocal ruin, and will give the sensation of a tight band around the throat.

It is very valuable to practise the echo effect. This is accomplished simply by singing "clearly" or brightly and vibrantly a tone, pronouncing the vowel sound well forward in its thinner and more brilliant form, changing the pronunciation, while holding the note, to the darker form of the vowel, made or pronounced "farther back." This alters the position of the tongue and fauces, making a larger space at the back of the pharynx, giving the tone a rather hollow sound, lacking in the brilliance of the normal tone, imitating the sound of the "echo." It is very easy of accomplishment, but very effective in performance. Of course, it is easier to produce this effect upon notes in the upper medium than upon lower notes, for these notes in the upper medium may be exaggerated in brightness and clarity because of their position, and the ensuing change of position of the vocal organs for the echo effect causes a great difference in the sound produced.

The trill has been open to much discussion regarding its production. I feel inclined to agree with many of the old school who frankly proclaimed that a singer either had the trill or did not have it, by natural gift. But of course the trill can be acquired by many who do not seem to possess it naturally. It should be borne in mind that the trill is the result of an oscillation of the larynx, which causes the "shake" or trill, and is not to be acquired by commencing with two adjacent notes, singing them slowly and then gradually more and more rapidly. This will never result in the real trill, but only in two notes sung at a more or less rapid speed. Such an effect is only a musical figure. The real trill is something very different, a real bird-like "warble." It is either readily learned, or it will cause the singer to become hoarse at each and every attempt. Unless the singer acquires the trill with much aptitude and facility, give it up. The best way to approach the trill is with the preparatory two notes, either from below or from above, changing this rather slow preparation suddenly into the real shake. In reality the larynx is somewhat "firmed," and the oscillation, while very slight, is very evident. The two pitches of the trill seem to be caused by this oscillation rather than by an actual alteration in the actions of the vocal cords and the arytenoids. This is apparently proved by the fact that if we try to trill on two notes at the interval of a major or minor third, it is practically impossible to make the real rapid shake. Also prepare the trill with triplets, accenting alternately the two notes of the trill as in Exercise 47.

Many singers think they trill by moving or shaking the jaw, a very prevalent and unsightly defect. Others think they trill when they are really sounding repetitions of the same note, instead of two notes. This results in the *Bockstriller* or goat-bleat, a ridiculous effect.

In general, do not try to trill on low notes at first. In the soprano the best notes for the practice of the trill are her middle D and upper G. Always let the attention of the singer rest upon the upper note, while trilling.

Do not confuse a violent stroke of the glottis, shock to the larynx, a "coughing" attack, with correct attack. The voice should be attacked cleanly and instantaneously without scooping and without a click or jar.

All the exercises may be sung with the vowels to advantage, preferably AH. The jaw should not move for L and N. It may close slightly for the vowel EE following AH or Ā. Do not exaggerate lip formation unduly. And always pronounce, pronounce, pronounce! Exercise 45 gives a suggestion for diction exercises. Many more may be invented to obtain fluency, but easy pieces are better and sustain the interest of the pupil.

It is only ethical to say that some of the exercises are original, but others given are either traditional, having been handed down by generations of teachers of singing, or they come from such men and women as G. B. Lamperti, F. Lamperti, Lablache, Sbriglia, Faure, Dubulle, Shaw, Marchesi, Jenny Lind, Manuel Garcia, and others.

A half-hour lesson is long enough, especially in the beginning. Later the lesson may be prolonged, but never until the pupil is the least fatigued. How many minutes or hours a pupil should sing each day is to be decided for each individual. One hour of honest endeavour is worth more than many hours of desultory effort. Every pupil should be taught to memorize without singing. It is a habit easily acquired if the pupil can read music fluently, and certainly we have a right to demand this of every singer. All songs, arias, exercises, should be sung by heart, and the pupil should stand at some distance from the piano. Let him always pay attention to his deportment, his position in standing, and also to facial expression, from the very first. It is often advantageous to indulge in two or three of the breathing gestures while inhaling, at intervals during the lesson.

Do not allow pupils to "parade" around the studio while singing. When they come to the study of operatic rôles, of course allow them to go through the action with the singing of the rôle.

Allow the pupil one day a week without singing. Some rest is necessary for everybody. Every teacher must have an inventive mind. The foregoing suggestions may help, but each teacher must experiment and invent new combinations of phonetics, using his own brains. I leave the rest to him.

*N. B.* In addition to the phonetics printed below, use those indicated in the text of the book.

Ah

Ah

Ah

Ah

Ah

Ah_____ Ah

Ah_____ Ah Ah Ah   Ah

Lah, lah lah lah,lah   lah lah lah,   *etc.*

Ah

Ah

36

Ah

37

Ah

Ah _____ Ah

Ah _____ Ah

38 *staccato*

Ah

39 *f* ———— *p*

Ah

Ah _____

41 **Messa di voce** (nota mentale)

Ah _____

voice ceases   breath support ceases

Ah _____

Ah _____

Ah _____

| Brah | Brā | Bree | Bro | Broo |
| Crah | Crā | Cree | Cro | Croo |
| Nah | Nā | Nee | No | Noo |
| Bah | Bā | Bee | Bo | Boo | *etc.*

Ah _____

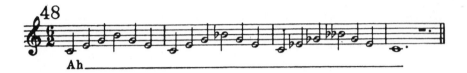

*(To the dominant — 5th — and return)*

# INDEX